TRIPLE TESTED
FOR YOUR SUCCESS EVERY TIME

For more than 50 years, *The Australian Women's Weekly* Test Kitchen has been creating marvellous recipes that come with a guarantee of success. First, the recipes always work – just follow the instructions and you too will get the results you see in the photographs. Second, and perhaps more importantly, they are delicious – created by experienced home economists and chefs, all triple-tested and, thanks to their straightforward instructions, easy to make.

Not all that long ago, the notion of a diet implied denial and deprivation — fortunately for us, times have changed. Along with our general understanding about healthier living, we've come to appreciate that a low-fat, well-balanced diet actually tastes better and delivers more energy than the kilojoule- and cholesterol-laden alternative.

And, in response to the increasingly hectic way most of us live, we've lightened up not just the content of our food, but also our approach to the way we serve and share it. We've included snacks and light meals that can be put together in minutes for family members who need good food fast when they come home briefly before dashing out again. As well, there are more substantial, but just as quick-and-easy to prepare, main courses and desserts for those special occasions when the whole household actually sits down together to eat!

Pamela Clark

FOOD EDITOR

contents

incidental exercise

We all *know* that exercise is good for us. It makes us feel good, reduces the risk of heart disease, lowers blood pressure, helps control weight, improves posture and helps to prevent osteoporosis. Yet many of us still don't exercise. **Why not?**

Perhaps we can't bear the thought of going to a gym with all those tanned and toned bodies; perhaps there's never time for a regular walk around the park; or perhaps, despite our best intentions, we just don't enjoy it enough to maintain an exercise regime. Well, here's the good news. You're probably doing more exercise than you think, just going about your daily life – and with very little effort, it's possible to do a whole lot more! This isn't a formal exercise routine, but a series of tips on how to increase your daily level of activity by making a few minor changes to your usual habits.

at home

• See household chores as an opportunity to burn a few kilojoules rather than just drudgery. Put on some lively music and dust or sweep in time to the beat.

• When there's time, mix ingredients by hand instead of using a mixer – it will take longer but it's marvellous for hand and arm strength and for relieving stress and frustration.

• Instead of setting the table all at once, walk around the table placing the forks, then around again placing the knives, and so forth.

• Don't use your clothes dryer (unless it's pouring, of course) – peg your washing out on the line in the fresh air, bending and stretching with each item.

• When watching television, don't just sit there: circle your feet or jiggle your arms and legs. Don't use the remote control: get up and change the channel or adjust the volume. During ad breaks, walk to the other end of the room or get up and stretch a few times.

• Instead of inviting a friend for coffee, suggest that you meet in a nearby park or garden and go for a gentle stroll while catching up with the latest gossip.

shopping

• Instead of repeatedly circling the car park looking for that perfect spot, park further away and walk the extra distance – you'll probably get to the shops faster anyway.

• Always walk your shopping trolley back to the store instead of leaving it in your car space.

• Use the stairs rather than lifts or escalators. If you can't find the stairs, walk up the escalator instead of just standing still for the ride.

• In the supermarket, to help keep your arms toned, gently push and pull your trolley backwards and forwards while walking down the aisles. You can also do this while waiting in the checkout queue.

Getty Images

Getty Images

at work

• Get off the bus one stop earlier on the way to and from work.

• Get out of the lift one stop before your usual floor and use the stairs. As you grow fitter you can gradually increase the number of flights of stairs.

• Leave some walking shoes at work and take a gentle stroll during your lunch break.

• Go window-shopping – it doesn't cost anything to look and will use up kilojoules as well as get you out of the office.

• Walk further than your usual sandwich shop and find a different place to eat.

• Place your wastepaper bin away from your desk and get up and walk to it when needed, resisting the urge to improve your aim!

in the car

• Turn on the radio and tap your hands or bop along to the music.

• If you drive an automatic car, instead of letting your left leg go to sleep during the trip, tap your foot in time to the music or circle your foot in each direction to stimulate the circulation.

• Train yourself to see a red traffic light as the perfect opportunity to work out a muscle or two – try pelvic floor exercises, or pushing and pulling on the steering wheel, or squeezing and releasing the wheel with your hands.

fit without a fuss

In the past it was thought that you had to exercise vigorously for a minimum of 30 minutes three to four times a week to get any benefits. However, this is not the case. Short duration activity, approximately 10 minutes each, that adds up to 30 minutes a day has been shown to help in decreasing blood pressure, blood cholesterol and body weight. This 30 minutes of accumulated exercise does not have to be vigorous, just at a level where your breathing is a little heavier than usual. And it doesn't need to involve joggers and bicycle pants – for instance, 30 minutes of gentle activity, such as sweeping the floor or gardening, will use up to 350 kilojoules. If you did this daily, it would add up to 124,000 kilojoules a year, which is the equivalent of 3kg of fat! Get out that broom ...

breakfast

From flavour- and vitamin-packed juice combos to more substantial hot dishes, this selection of breakfast recipes will make the most important meal of the day also one of the most enjoyable.

buckwheat pancakes with caramelised banana

PREPARATION TIME 10 MINUTES (plus refrigeration time) • COOKING TIME 20 MINUTES

The seeds of the buckwheat plant are ground into the flour that is the essential ingredient in Japanese soba, Russian blini and delicious pancakes such as these.

1/4 cup (35g) self-raising flour
1/4 cup (35g) buckwheat flour
1 tablespoon caster sugar
1/4 teaspoon ground cinnamon
1 egg
3/4 cup (180ml) skim milk
20g butter
1/4 cup (50g) firmly packed
   brown sugar
4 medium bananas (800g),
   sliced thickly
2 tablespoons water

1 Combine flours, caster sugar and cinnamon in medium bowl; gradually whisk in combined egg and milk until smooth. Cover; refrigerate 30 minutes.

2 Meanwhile, melt butter in large frying pan; add brown sugar, cook, stirring, until dissolved. Add banana and the water; cook, uncovered, stirring occasionally, about 2 minutes or until banana is caramelised.

3 Pour 1/4 cup batter into heated 20cm non-stick frying pan; cook pancake until browned both sides. Repeat with remaining batter; this quantity of batter will make four pancakes. Cover to keep warm.

4 Just before serving, halve each pancake; divide halves among serving plates. Spoon banana mixture onto each half, fold to enclose filling, drizzle with caramel.

SERVES 4

per serving 6.1g fat; 1285kJ
serving suggestion These pancakes also make a lovely dessert.
tips Fresh strawberries may be used as a filling instead of caramelised bananas.
Dust pancakes with icing sugar mixture before serving.

fruit salad with honey yogurt

PREPARATION TIME 15 MINUTES

We have the Greeks to thank for the serendipitous combination of yogurt and honey, and the benevolence of the Australian tropics for the combination of fruits. You need only small quantities of pineapple and rockmelon for this recipe, so buy the smallest ones you can find. Two passionfruit will supply the right amount of pulp.

³/₄ cup (210g) low-fat yogurt
2 tablespoons honey
200g peeled, coarsely
**   chopped pineapple**
200g seeded, peeled, coarsely
**   chopped rockmelon**
250g strawberries, halved
250g blueberries
1 large banana (230g),
**   sliced thinly**
2 tablespoons passionfruit pulp
2 teaspoons lime juice
12 fresh mint leaves

1 Combine yogurt and honey in small bowl.

2 Just before serving, combine remaining ingredients in large bowl; serve with honey yogurt.

SERVES 4

per serving 2g fat; 749kJ

tips Lime juice not only adds flavour to this recipe but also prevents the banana from discolouring.

Honey yogurt can be made a day ahead; store, covered, in refrigerator.

pineapple and mint frappé

PREPARATION TIME 20 MINUTES

The word frappé is a French description for frozen or chilled drinks and dishes.

**1 large pineapple (2kg),
  peeled, chopped coarsely**
40 ice cubes, crushed
**1 tablespoon finely chopped
  fresh mint leaves**

1 Blend or process pineapple until smooth; transfer to large jug.

2 Stir in ice and mint; pour into serving glasses.

SERVES 4 (MAKES 1.5 LITRES)

per 375ml serving
0.3g fat; 412kJ

tips Pineapple can be processed several hours ahead. Refrigerate, covered, until ready to combine with ice and serve.

You can crush the ice in a blender or food processor.

fresh berry frappé

PREPARATION TIME 10 MINUTES

You can also use frozen berries for this recipe. Experiment with other berries – strawberries, blackberries, boysenberries – and adjust combinations to your taste.

300g blueberries
250g raspberries
40 ice cubes, crushed
1/2 cup (125ml) fresh
  orange juice

1 Blend or process berries until just smooth. Push berry puree through fine sieve into large bowl; discard solids in sieve.

2 Stir in ice and juice; spoon into serving glasses.

SERVES 4 (MAKES 3½ CUPS)

per 220ml serving
0.4g fat; 293kJ

tips Depending on the sweetness of the berries, you may need to add sugar.

You can crush the ice in a blender or food processor.

mushroom and parsley omelette

PREPARATION TIME 10 MINUTES • COOKING TIME 10 MINUTES

4 eggs, beaten lightly
6 egg whites
**500g swiss brown mushrooms,
  sliced thinly**
**1/3 cup loosely packed,
  coarsely chopped fresh
  flat-leaf parsley**

1 Whisk beaten egg with egg whites in medium bowl.

2 Cook mushrooms in heated non-stick 20cm frying pan, stirring, until tender. Place mushrooms with parsley in small bowl.

3 Return pan to heat, add a quarter of the egg mixture; cook, tilting pan, over medium heat until almost set. Place a quarter of the mushroom mixture evenly over half of the omelette; fold omelette over to enclose filling, slide onto serving plate. Repeat with remaining egg and mushroom mixtures to make four omelettes in total.

SERVES 4

per serving 5.6g fat; 527kJ
serving suggestion Serve with thick slices of toasted sourdough.
tip Basil can be substituted for parsley.

banana smoothie

PREPARATION TIME 5 MINUTES

A health-food craze that began in San Francisco in the 1980s has blenders working overtime around the world.

2 cups (500ml) skim milk
2 medium bananas (400g),
  chopped coarsely
¹/₂ cup (140g) low-fat yogurt
1 tablespoon honey
1 tablespoon wheat germ
¹/₄ teaspoon ground cinnamon

Blend or process ingredients until smooth.

SERVES 4 (MAKES 1 LITRE)

per 250ml serving 0.9g fat; 633kJ

tip Use frozen bananas or add ice cubes to blender for a thicker smoothie.

porridge with apple compote

PREPARATION TIME 10 MINUTES • COOKING TIME 10 MINUTES

*There can be few things as comforting or nutritious as a warming bowl of porridge. Here, it's given
a natural flavour enhancer with the addition of gently cooked apples, tasting of cinnamon.*

2 medium apples (300g)
1/4 cup (55g) caster sugar
1/4 teaspoon ground cinnamon
1/4 cup (60ml) water
8 dried apricots
1 tablespoon sultanas
1 cup (90g) rolled oats
1 cup (250ml) skim milk
1 1/2 cups (375ml) boiling water
2 tablespoons brown sugar

1 Peel, core and slice apples thickly; combine apple with caster sugar,
cinnamon and the water in medium saucepan. Cook, stirring, over low
heat until sugar dissolves. Bring apple mixture to a boil, reduce heat;
simmer, uncovered, 5 minutes. Add apricots and sultanas; simmer,
uncovered, about 5 minutes or until apple is tender.

2 Meanwhile, combine oats, milk and the boiling water in another medium
saucepan; bring to a boil. Reduce heat; simmer, uncovered, about
5 minutes or until mixture thickens.

3 Serve porridge with apple compote, sprinkled with brown sugar.

SERVES 4

per serving 2.1g fat; 1019kJ

tip Any other dried fruit, such as prunes, pears or peaches, could be
used instead of the apricots.

grilled mango and ricotta with english muffins

PREPARATION TIME 10 MINUTES • COOKING TIME 5 MINUTES

You need two passionfruit for this recipe.

1 cup (200g) low-fat ricotta cheese
3/4 cup (210g) low-fat tropical yogurt
2 small mangoes (600g)
2 white english muffins
2 tablespoons passionfruit pulp

1 Whisk cheese and yogurt together in medium bowl until mixture is smooth.

2 Slice cheeks from mangoes; remove skin, cut each cheek in half.

3 Cook mango on heated oiled grill plate (or grill or barbecue) until browned both sides.

4 Just before serving, split muffins; toast both sides. Place half a muffin on each serving plate; top with cheese mixture and mango, drizzle with passionfruit pulp.

SERVES 4

per serving 5.2g fat; 1030kJ

serving suggestion Drizzle some maple syrup over the mangoes, if extra sweetness is desired.

tip If mangoes are unavailable, you could substitute pineapple.

grapefruit passion

PREPARATION TIME 10 MINUTES

Give a cold a healthy blast of vitamin C with this drink. Originating in Brazil, the passionfruit was named by Jesuit priests for the appearance of the flower, which brought to mind the crucifixion and the crown of thorns. You need about 24 passionfruit to get 2 cups (500ml) of the pulp.

4 medium ruby grapefruit (1.7kg), peeled, chopped coarsely
300g raspberries
2 cups (500ml) passionfruit pulp
1 teaspoon sugar

Push fruit through juice extractor. Add sugar; stir to combine.

SERVES 4 (MAKES 1 LITRE)

per 250ml serving 1.2g fat; 843kJ

tip You can use oranges or mandarins instead of grapefruit, if you prefer a sweeter juice.

vegetable juice

PREPARATION TIME 10 MINUTES

2 medium beetroot (600g), trimmed, quartered
3 trimmed celery sticks (225g)
3 medium carrots (360g), halved lengthways
2 small apples (260g), quartered
2 medium oranges (480g), peeled, quartered

Push ingredients through juice extractor. Stir to combine.

SERVES 4 (MAKES 1 LITRE)

per 250ml serving 0.4g fat; 579kJ

tip For a more tart drink, you could use one large grapefruit (500g) in place of the oranges.

tropical delight

PREPARATION TIME 10 MINUTES

You need about 400g of peeled and chopped pineapple for this recipe.

1 small pineapple (800g), peeled, chopped coarsely
4 medium apples (600g), chopped coarsely
2 medium oranges (480g), peeled, chopped coarsely

Push fruit through juice extractor. Stir to combine.

SERVES 4 (MAKES 1 LITRE)

per 250ml serving 0.3g fat; 512kJ

melon mania

PREPARATION TIME 10 MINUTES

Capture the essence of summer with this refreshing combination. You need a piece of a small round watermelon weighing about 1.5kg and half of both a medium rockmelon and a honeydew melon for this recipe.

600g seeded, peeled, coarsely chopped rockmelon
600g seeded, peeled, coarsely chopped honeydew melon
1kg seeded, peeled, coarsely chopped watermelon
250g strawberries, halved

Push fruit through juice extractor. Stir to combine.

SERVES 4 (MAKES 1 LITRE)

per 250ml serving 1.1g fat; 603kJ

tip Refrigerate the fruit before processing so that the flavours are at their sharpest.

If you don't own a juice extractor, blend or process the fruit for these drinks until pureed then push the mixture through a fine sieve into a large jug.

juices

low-fat toasted muesli

PREPARATION TIME 10 MINUTES
COOKING TIME 30 MINUTES (plus standing time)

The word muesli translates from German as mixture, liberally interpreted by the Swiss as a wholesome flavour-packed combination of cereals, nuts, fruit, and honey or sugar.

2 cups (180g) rolled oats
1 cup (100g) triticale flakes
1 cup (60g) unprocessed bran
1 cup (130g) barley flakes
1 cup (140g) soy wholegrain flakes
1/2 cup (60g) rice flakes
1/2 cup (65g) rye flakes
1/4 cup (60ml) macadamia oil
1/2 cup (175g) honey
1/3 cup (55g) pepitas
2 tablespoons linseeds
2 tablespoons sunflower seed kernels
1 cup (150g) coarsely chopped dried apricots
1 cup (90g) coarsely chopped dried apples
1 cup (160g) seeded, coarsely chopped dried dates
1 cup (160g) sultanas

1 Preheat oven to moderate.

2 Combine cereals, oil and honey in large shallow baking dish; toast, uncovered, in moderate oven, about 30 minutes or until browned lightly, stirring at least three times during cooking time. Cool toasted cereal 10 minutes, stir in remaining ingredients.

MAKES 1.5kg (12 CUPS)

per 1/2 cup (60g) serving 7.2g fat; 973kJ
serving suggestion Serve with skim milk and stone fruit or berries.
tip Store in airtight container in refrigerator for up to 3 months.

tropical fruit lassi

PREPARATION TIME 15 MINUTES

The lassi is a frothy yogurt or
buttermilk drink that has migrated into
many cuisines from its home country,
India. You need only 100g of both
peeled and chopped pineapple and
rockmelon for this recipe, so buy the
smallest ones you can find – and eat
what's left as part of a fruit salad later.

1 cup (280g) low-fat yogurt
1/2 cup (125ml) water
100g seeded, peeled, coarsely
    chopped rockmelon
100g peeled, coarsely
    chopped pineapple
1 small mango (300g), peeled,
    chopped coarsely
100g strawberries, halved
1 tablespoon caster sugar
6 ice cubes

Blend or process ingredients
until smooth.

SERVES 4 (MAKES 1 LITRE)

per 250ml serving
1.4g fat; 487kJ

tip Vary the fruit according to
the season and your preferences.

day-before muffins

PREPARATION TIME 15 MINUTES (plus refrigeration time) • COOKING TIME 30 MINUTES

When you have overnight guests or friends coming for breakfast, prepare ahead for a breakfast of muffins fresh from the oven! The muffin batter is partially made the day before and refrigerated overnight, needing only a few more minutes of preparation before baking and serving.

$^2/_3$ **cup (100g) coarsely chopped dried apricots**

$^1/_2$ **cup (95g) coarsely chopped dried figs**

$1^1/_3$ **cups (95g) All-Bran breakfast cereal**

$1^1/_2$ **cups (375ml) skim milk**

$1^1/_4$ **cups (250g) firmly packed brown sugar**

$1^1/_2$ **tablespoons golden syrup**

$1^1/_4$ **cups (185g) self-raising flour**

$^1/_2$ **cup (60g) pecans, chopped coarsely**

1 Combine apricot, fig, cereal, milk, sugar and syrup in large bowl; mix well. Cover; refrigerate overnight.

2 Preheat oven to moderately hot. Lightly grease four holes only of a six-hole Texas ($^3/_4$ cup/180ml) muffin pan.

3 Stir flour and nuts into apricot mixture. Spoon mixture into prepared muffin pan; bake in moderately hot oven about 30 minutes. Serve muffins hot or cold.

SERVES 4

per serving 11.1g fat; 2941kJ

serving suggestion Serve with fresh fruit jam or top with dried apricots; dust with icing sugar, if desired.

tip Muffins can be frozen for up to 2 months.

rösti with ham and cherry tomatoes

PREPARATION TIME 15 MINUTES • COOKING TIME 25 MINUTES

200g shaved light ham
4 large potatoes (1.2kg), grated coarsely
1 egg white, beaten lightly
cooking-oil spray
200g cherry tomatoes
2 green onions, trimmed, chopped coarsely

1 Preheat oven to hot.

2 Place ham on oven tray; cook in hot oven, uncovered, until browned lightly.

3 Meanwhile, combine potato and egg white in large bowl; divide into four portions. Spray heated large non-stick frying pan with cooking-oil spray; cook one portion of potato mixture, forming into flat pancake shape while cooking, until browned both sides and cooked through. Repeat with remaining portions. Cover rösti to keep warm.

4 Cook tomatoes in same pan until just beginning to soften. Serve rösti topped with ham, tomato and onion.

SERVES 4

per serving 2.9g fat; 1121kJ
tip Wilted baby spinach leaves can also be served with these rösti.

dipping in

Indulge yourself with this collection of figure-friendly dips, served with plain water crackers, crisped flat bread or oven-baked bagel chips.

herb ricotta dip

PREPARATION TIME 15 MINUTES

2 tablespoons skim milk
150g packaged low-fat cream cheese
100g low-fat ricotta cheese
2 cloves garlic, quartered
2 teaspoons lemon juice
1 tablespoon coarsely chopped
    fresh chives
1 tablespoon coarsely chopped
    fresh flat-leaf parsley
1 tablespoon coarsely chopped
    fresh thyme leaves
1 tablespoon coarsely chopped capers

Blend or process milk, cheeses, garlic and juice until smooth. Stir in herbs and capers.

MAKES 1¹/₄ CUPS

per tablespoon 2.3g fat; 124kJ

serving suggestion Serve with vegetable sticks, crackers, or thinly sliced toasted bread stick.

tip Dip can be made 3 hours ahead of time and refrigerated, covered. Alternatively, make cheese mixture the day before and stir in herbs just before serving.

tomato salsa

PREPARATION TIME 15 MINUTES

3 medium tomatoes (570g), seeded, chopped finely
1 small avocado (200g), chopped finely
1 medium red onion (170g), chopped finely
2 red thai chillies, seeded, chopped finely
2 tablespoons coarsely chopped fresh coriander leaves
130g canned corn kernels, rinsed, drained
1 tablespoon lemon juice

Combine ingredients in medium bowl.

MAKES 2 CUPS

per tablespoon 1.4g fat; 81kJ

serving suggestion Serve with baked flour tortilla wedges or corn chips.

sweet chilli dip

PREPARATION TIME 5 MINUTES

250g softened packaged low-fat cream cheese
¼ cup (60ml) mild sweet chilli sauce
1 tablespoon coarsely chopped fresh coriander leaves

Combine ingredients in small bowl; mix well.

MAKES 1¼ CUPS

per tablespoon 2.9g fat; 153kJ

serving suggestion Serve with crackers or vegetable sticks.

light meals

Whether you want a quick lunch or a light supper – or just to keep the munchies at bay in between – this appealing selection of low-fat soups, sandwiches, stir-fries and salads should keep you satisfied.

vegetable and red lentil soup

PREPARATION TIME 5 MINUTES • COOKING TIME 25 MINUTES

Used since prehistoric times, lentils are an excellent source of protein, fibre and B vitamins. As the Hindu proverb says: "Rice is good, but lentils are my life."

2 tablespoons mild curry paste
400g can tomatoes
3 cups (750ml) chicken stock
1 large carrot (180g), chopped finely
2 trimmed celery sticks (150g), chopped finely
1 medium potato (200g), chopped finely
1 large zucchini (150g), chopped finely
3/4 cup (150g) red lentils
1/2 cup (60g) frozen peas
1/3 cup (80ml) light coconut milk
2 tablespoons coarsely chopped fresh coriander leaves

1 Cook curry paste in heated large saucepan, stirring, about 1 minute or until fragrant. Add undrained crushed tomatoes, stock, carrot, celery, potato and zucchini; bring to a boil. Reduce heat; simmer, covered, 5 minutes.

2 Add lentils to soup mixture; return to a boil. Reduce heat; simmer, uncovered, about 10 minutes or until lentils are just tender. Add peas; return to a boil. Reduce heat; simmer soup mixture, uncovered, until peas are just tender.

3 Remove soup from heat; stir in remaining ingredients.

SERVES 6

per serving 4.4g fat; 696kJ

serving suggestion Accompany with pappadums puffed in a microwave oven and a small bowl of raita (finely chopped cucumber combined with low-fat yogurt).

tip A hotter curry paste or some finely chopped chilli can be added to boost the flavour.

chicken broth with rice noodles

PREPARATION TIME 15 MINUTES • COOKING TIME 25 MINUTES (plus cooling time)

You'll find a version of this popular soup in most Asian cuisines; this one has a Thai accent.

1.5 litres (6 cups) chicken stock
2 cups (500ml) water
50g piece ginger, sliced thinly
350g chicken breast fillets
500g fresh rice noodles
1/4 cup (60ml) lime juice
1 tablespoon fish sauce
4 green onions, chopped coarsely
2 red thai chillies, seeded,
  sliced thinly
2 tablespoons coarsely chopped
  fresh coriander leaves
1 cup (80g) bean sprouts

1 Bring stock, the water and ginger to a boil in large saucepan. Add chicken, return to a boil, reduce heat; simmer, covered, about 15 minutes or until chicken is cooked through. Remove chicken; cool 10 minutes then shred coarsely.

2 Return broth mixture to a boil; add noodles, juice and sauce. Reduce heat; simmer, stirring, until noodles are just tender.

3 Add chicken and remaining ingredients to broth; stir over heat until hot.

SERVES 4

per serving 7.4g fat; 1711kJ

serving suggestion Serve with wedges of lime and follow with a selection of tropical fruit.

tips Coarsely chopped leafy green Chinese vegetables, such as choy sum or water spinach, can be added to this broth.

Dried rice noodles, or the thicker rice stick noodles, can be substituted for fresh noodles; they need to be soaked in boiling water for about 5 minutes and drained before being added to the stock.

pea and potato soup

PREPARATION TIME 10 MINUTES • COOKING TIME 30 MINUTES (plus cooling time)

Leek and potato are natural allies when teamed in a satisfying winter soup. Take care to wash the leeks well under cold water to remove any grit.

3 cups (750ml) chicken stock
2 medium leeks (700g),
  sliced thinly
1 clove garlic, crushed
2 medium potatoes (400g),
  chopped coarsely
4 cups (500g) frozen peas
3 cups (750ml) water
2 tablespoons finely shredded
  fresh mint leaves

1 Heat 2 tablespoons of the stock in large saucepan, add leek and garlic; cook, stirring, about 10 minutes or until leek is soft.

2 Add remaining stock, potato, peas and the water to pan; bring to a boil. Reduce heat; simmer, covered, about 15 minutes or until vegetables are tender. Cool 10 minutes.

3 Blend or process soup, in batches, until smooth.

4 Return soup to same cleaned pan; stir over heat until hot. Stir in mint just before serving.

SERVES 4

per serving 1.8g fat; 822kJ

serving suggestion Herb scones or damper would make a good accompaniment for this soup.

beef and noodle stir-fry

PREPARATION TIME 15 MINUTES (plus soaking time)
COOKING TIME 20 MINUTES

Rice stick noodles, also known as sen lek (Thai) and ho fun (Chinese), are wide, flat noodles made from rice flour. They must be softened by being soaked in boiling water before use.

250g rice stick noodles
2 teaspoons peanut oil
500g beef eye fillet, sliced thinly
1 clove garlic, crushed
1 tablespoon finely chopped lemon grass
2 red thai chillies, seeded, sliced thinly
1/3 cup (80ml) lime juice
1 tablespoon fish sauce
100g baby rocket leaves
1 cup (80g) bean sprouts
1/2 cup loosely packed fresh coriander leaves
1/2 cup loosely packed fresh mint leaves
3 green onions, sliced thinly
1 lebanese cucumber (130g), seeded, sliced thinly

1 Place noodles in large heatproof bowl, cover with boiling water; stand 5 minutes or until tender, drain.

2 Heat half of the oil in wok or large frying pan; cook beef, in batches, until browned.

3 Heat remaining oil in wok; cook garlic, lemon grass and chilli until fragrant. Return beef to wok with juice and sauce, stir-fry until heated through. Add noodles, stir-fry until combined. Stir in remaining ingredients; serve immediately.

SERVES 4

per serving 9.5g fat; 1534kJ

serving suggestion Serve with wedges of lime and a bowl of finely chopped chilli so that diners can adjust flavours according to their taste.

tip You can substitute baby spinach leaves, chinese water spinach or baby tat soi leaves for the rocket.

steak sandwich

PREPARATION TIME 15 MINUTES • COOKING TIME 15 MINUTES

Mesclun is a mixture of various baby salad leaves; substitute any single lettuce variety if you prefer.
Beef rib-eye is also called scotch fillet by some butchers.

**2 small leeks (400g),
 sliced thinly**
1 tablespoon brown sugar
1/4 cup (60ml) dry white wine
1 tablespoon seeded mustard
**2 medium zucchini (240g),
 sliced thinly**
**2 baby eggplants (120g),
 sliced thinly**
**2 medium tomatoes (380g),
 sliced thickly**
4 x 100g beef rib-eye steaks
8 slices white bread
50g mesclun

1 Cook leek, with about 2 tablespoons of water to prevent it sticking, in medium non-stick frying pan over low heat, stirring, until softened. Add sugar, wine and mustard; cook, stirring, about 10 minutes or until leek is browned and liquid evaporates.

2 Meanwhile, cook zucchini, eggplant and tomato on oiled grill plate (or grill or barbecue) until vegetables are browned all over and just tender. Keep warm.

3 Cook beef on heated oiled grill plate (or grill or barbecue) until browned both sides and cooked as desired.

4 Toast bread lightly. Sandwich each steak, with a quarter each of the vegetables and mesclun, between two pieces of toast.

SERVES 4

per serving 8g fat; 2205kJ
serving suggestion Serve with oven-baked potato wedges.
tip Leek may be cooked longer to caramelise it if you prefer.

creamy mushroom pasta

PREPARATION TIME 15 MINUTES • COOKING TIME 15 MINUTES

Skim milk keeps the fat count down but the creamy taste intact. You can use any kind of short pasta you like – penne, rigatoni – in place of the shells.

375g shell pasta
1/4 cup (60ml) vegetable stock
1 clove garlic, crushed
500g button mushrooms,
  sliced thickly
1 cup (125g) frozen peas
4 green onions, sliced thinly
1 litre (4 cups) skim milk
1 1/2 tablespoons cornflour
2 tablespoons water
1/4 cup coarsely chopped fresh
  flat-leaf parsley
1 tablespoon seeded mustard
1/2 cup (40g) finely grated
  parmesan cheese
2 tablespoons finely chopped
  fresh chives

1 Cook pasta in large saucepan of boiling water, uncovered, until just tender; drain, keep warm.

2 Bring stock to a boil in same cleaned saucepan; cook garlic and mushrooms, stirring, until mushrooms soften and liquid evaporates. Stir in peas and half of the onion; cook, stirring, until onion softens.

3 Add milk and blended cornflour and water; cook, stirring, over low heat until sauce boils and thickens slightly.

4 Remove sauce from heat; stir in pasta, remaining onion, parsley, mustard and cheese. Serve sprinkled with chives.

SERVES 4

per serving 3.8g fat; 1500kJ

serving suggestion Serve with crusty sourdough bread.

tips Toss pasta through sauce just before serving – it will soak up all the sauce if tossed too early.

Swiss brown, flat or oyster mushrooms could be used instead of button.

pork rice-paper rolls

PREPARATION TIME 30 MINUTES • COOKING TIME 5 MINUTES

When soaked in hot water, Vietnamese rice-paper sheets (banh trang) make pliable wrappers for a host of fillings. You will need a small chinese cabbage for this recipe.

350g minced pork
1 clove garlic, crushed
1 teaspoon grated fresh ginger
1 teaspoon five-spice powder
350g finely shredded chinese cabbage
4 green onions, sliced thinly
1 tablespoon soy sauce
1/4 cup (60ml) oyster sauce
1/4 cup tightly packed, coarsely chopped fresh coriander leaves
12 x 22cm rice paper sheets
1/4 cup (60ml) sweet chilli sauce
2 tablespoons lime juice

1 Cook pork, garlic, ginger and spice in large non-stick frying pan, stirring, until pork is changed in colour and cooked through.

2 Add cabbage, onion, soy sauce, oyster sauce and 2 tablespoons of the coriander to pan; cook, stirring, until cabbage is just wilted.

3 Place one sheet of rice paper in medium bowl of warm water until softened slightly; lift sheet carefully from water, place on board, pat dry with absorbent paper. Place a twelfth of the filling mixture in centre of sheet; fold in sides, roll top to bottom to enclose filling. Repeat with remaining rice paper sheets and filling.

4 Place rolls in single layer in large steamer set over large saucepan of simmering water; steam, covered, about 5 minutes or until just heated through. Serve rolls with dipping sauce made with combined remaining coriander, chilli sauce and juice.

SERVES 4

per serving 7.1g fat; 1041kJ

serving suggestion These rolls could be served as a substantial starter before a main course of fried rice (page 36) or a bowl of chicken broth with rice noodles (page 28).

tip Rolls can be prepared a day ahead; store, covered, in refrigerator.

fried rice

PREPARATION TIME 10 MINUTES • COOKING TIME 10 MINUTES

Ketjap manis is a thick, sweet soy sauce that originated in Indonesia. You need to cook 1 cup (200g) long-grain white rice several hours or a day before making this recipe; spread the still-warm cooked rice on a tray to cool, then cover and refrigerate until required.

2 eggs, beaten lightly
cooking-oil spray
120g baby corn, halved
1 trimmed celery stick (75g),
  chopped finely
1 small red capsicum (150g),
  chopped finely
2 cloves garlic, crushed
140g light ham, chopped coarsely
3 cups cooked long-grain
  white rice
1 tablespoon ketjap manis
4 green onions, sliced thinly

1 Pour egg into heated medium non-stick pan; cook, tilting pan, over medium heat until just set. Roll omelette then slice thinly; reserve.

2 Spray heated wok or large frying pan lightly with cooking-oil spray; stir-fry corn and celery 2 minutes. Add capsicum, garlic and ham; stir-fry 2 minutes. Add rice and ketjap manis; stir-fry until heated through. Stir in onion and omelette; serve immediately.

SERVES 4

per serving 4.8g fat; 1155kJ
serving suggestion Serve with steamed greens or stir-fried vegetables.
tip A little chopped fresh chilli can be added for a hint of spice.

penne with tomato salsa and tuna

PREPARATION TIME 15 MINUTES • COOKING TIME 20 MINUTES

The Italian name of this pasta means pens, a reference to the nib-like, pointy ends of each piece of pasta. Penne comes in both smooth (lisce) or ridged (rigate) versions, and a variety of sizes.

375g penne
3 medium tomatoes (570g),
   seeded, chopped finely
1 medium red onion (170g),
   chopped finely
2 cloves garlic, crushed
1/4 cup firmly packed, torn fresh
   basil leaves
425g can tuna in brine,
   drained, flaked
1/4 cup (60ml) balsamic vinegar

1 Cook pasta in large saucepan of boiling water, uncovered, until just tender; drain, keep warm.

2 Combine tomato, onion, garlic, basil, tuna, pasta and vinegar in large bowl; toss to combine.

SERVES 4

per serving 3.8g fat; 1930kJ

serving suggestion Serve with ciabatta bread and a mixed green salad.

tip You can substitute any pasta for the penne in this recipe.

rice with mushrooms and spinach

PREPARATION TIME 10 MINUTES • COOKING TIME 25 MINUTES

A simple covered cooking method replaces the usual labour-intensive non-stop stirring required in more traditional risottos. Best results will be achieved by using arborio rice, but you can use any medium-grain rice, such as calrose.

3 cups (750ml) vegetable stock
1/4 cup (60ml) dry white wine
1 tablespoon finely grated lemon rind
1 medium brown onion (150g), chopped finely
2 cloves garlic, crushed
250g swiss brown mushrooms, halved
150g button mushrooms, halved
1 1/2 cups (300g) medium-grain white rice
2 tablespoons lemon juice
1 cup (250ml) water
100g baby spinach leaves, torn
1/2 cup (40g) finely grated parmesan cheese
2 tablespoons shredded fresh basil leaves

1 Heat 1 tablespoon of the stock with wine and rind in large saucepan; cook onion and garlic, stirring, until onion softens. Add mushrooms; cook, stirring, 5 minutes.

2 Stir in rice, juice, the water and remaining stock. Bring to a boil, reduce heat; simmer, covered, about 20 minutes or until rice is tender.

3 Just before serving, stir in spinach, cheese and basil.

SERVES 4

per serving 4.9g fat; 1603kJ

serving suggestion Olive or sourdough bread and a balsamic-dressed mesclun salad turn this dish into a meal.

tip Flat-leaf parsley can be substituted for the basil.

rosemary lamb open sandwich

PREPARATION TIME 5 MINUTES (plus refrigeration time) • COOKING TIME 15 MINUTES

4 lamb fillets (320g)
2 cloves garlic, crushed
1/4 cup (60ml) lemon juice
2 tablespoons fresh
  rosemary leaves
1 tablespoon seeded mustard
2 small tomatoes (260g)
250g asparagus, halved
4 slices light rye bread
100g butter lettuce,
  chopped coarsely

1 In a small bowl, combine lamb, garlic, juice, rosemary and mustard, cover; refrigerate 3 hours or overnight.

2 Cut each tomato into six wedges. Cook tomato and asparagus, in batches, on heated oiled grill plate (or grill or barbecue) until browned lightly and just tender. Toast bread both sides.

3 Drain lamb; discard marinade. Cook lamb on same heated grill plate (or grill or barbecue) until browned and cooked as desired. Cover; stand 5 minutes before slicing thickly.

4 Place one slice of the toast on each serving plate; top each slice with equal amounts of lettuce, tomato, asparagus and lamb.

SERVES 4

per serving 4.5g fat; 849kJ

serving suggestion Dollop a spoonful of guacamole or low-fat mayonnaise, spiked with crushed garlic, on each sandwich.

tip You can substitute toasted sourdough or ciabatta for the rye bread.

pasta and herb salad with lamb fillets

PREPARATION TIME 20 MINUTES • COOKING TIME 10 MINUTES (plus standing time)

This salad can be served warm or cold. You can substitute your favourite pasta for the farfalle.

375g farfalle
250g yellow teardrop
  tomatoes, halved
1 medium red onion (170g),
  sliced thinly
50g rocket leaves
¼ cup loosely packed, finely
  shredded fresh basil leaves
1 tablespoon fresh thyme leaves
400g lamb fillets
2 cloves garlic, crushed
1 tablespoon seeded mustard
¼ cup (60ml) balsamic vinegar

1 Cook pasta in large saucepan of boiling water, uncovered, until just tender; drain.

2 Combine tomato, onion, rocket, basil and thyme in large bowl.

3 Rub lamb all over with combined garlic and mustard; cook on heated oiled grill plate (or grill or barbecue) until browned both sides and cooked as desired. Stand 5 minutes; slice thinly.

4 Add pasta, lamb and vinegar to vegetables; toss to combine.

SERVES 4

per serving 4.9g fat; 1910kJ

serving suggestion A crusty bread is a good partner for this salad. To complete a terrific outdoor lunch, serve ricotta and berry trifle (page 107) or caramelised oranges with ice-cream (page 111) for dessert.

moroccan lamb with couscous

PREPARATION TIME 15 MINUTES (plus refrigeration time)
COOKING TIME 15 MINUTES

Yogurt is used in both the marinade and as the sauce for the lamb in this recipe.

8 lamb fillets (700g)
1 tablespoon ground cumin
1 tablespoon ground coriander
1 teaspoon ground cinnamon
3/4 cup (210g) low-fat yogurt
11/2 cups (300g) couscous
11/2 cups (375ml) boiling water
1 teaspoon peanut oil
1/3 cup (50g) dried currants
2 teaspoons finely grated lemon rind
2 teaspoons lemon juice
1/4 cup firmly packed, coarsely chopped fresh coriander leaves

1 Combine lamb, spices and 1/3 cup of the yogurt in medium bowl, cover; refrigerate 3 hours or overnight.

2 Cook lamb on heated oiled grill plate (or grill or barbecue) until browned and cooked as desired. Cover; stand 5 minutes, slice thinly.

3 Meanwhile, combine couscous, water and oil in large heatproof bowl, cover; stand 5 minutes or until liquid is absorbed, fluffing with fork occasionally. Stir in currants, rind, juice and fresh coriander; toss with fork to combine.

4 Serve lamb with couscous; drizzle with remaining yogurt.

SERVES 4

per serving 9.3g fat; 2193kJ

serving suggestion Serve with harissa, the fiery North African condiment.

tip You could substitute some finely chopped preserved lemon for the lemon juice and rind in the couscous.

chicken, noodle and oyster-mushroom stir-fry

PREPARATION TIME 15 MINUTES • COOKING TIME 15 MINUTES

You will need about 800g of broccoli for this recipe. Hokkien (or stir-fry) noodles are sold in cryovac packages in the refrigerated section of your supermarket.

500g hokkien noodles
500g chicken thigh fillets,
  chopped coarsely
1 clove garlic, crushed
200g broccoli florets
150g oyster mushrooms, halved
1 medium red onion (170g),
  sliced thinly
200g snow peas, halved
1/4 cup (60ml) oyster sauce

1 Rinse noodles under hot water; drain. Transfer to large bowl; separate noodles with fork.

2 Stir-fry chicken in heated lightly oiled wok or large frying pan, in batches, until browned all over and cooked through.

3 Stir-fry garlic, broccoli, mushrooms and onion in same pan until onion just softens. Return chicken to wok with noodles, snow peas and sauce; stir-fry until vegetables are just tender.

SERVES 4

per serving 10.9g fat; 2360kJ

serving suggestion Serve with a side dish of chopped fresh chilli or sambal oelek to add heat to the noodles.

sweet chilli chicken with rice

PREPARATION TIME 10 MINUTES (plus refrigeration time) • COOKING TIME 15 MINUTES

Garlic, lemon grass and sweet chilli sauce lend a Thai accent to this recipe.

2 teaspoons grated fresh ginger
3 cloves garlic, crushed
**1 tablespoon finely chopped fresh
    lemon grass**
1/4 cup (60ml) sweet chilli sauce
1/4 cup (60ml) lime juice
**1/2 cup loosely packed, coarsely
    chopped fresh coriander leaves**
**4 single chicken breast
    fillets (680g)**
**3/4 cup (150g) long-grain
    white rice**
1 cup (250ml) chicken stock
2 teaspoons cornflour

1 Combine ginger, garlic, lemon grass, sauce, juice and half of the coriander
   with chicken in large bowl, cover; refrigerate 3 hours or overnight.

2 Drain chicken over large bowl; reserve marinade. Cook chicken,
   uncovered, in heated large non-stick frying pan until browned both sides
   and cooked through; slice chicken thickly.

3 Boil, steam or microwave rice until just tender; drain, if necessary,
   then stir in remaining coriander.

4 Meanwhile, blend 2 tablespoons of the stock with cornflour in small jug;
   place remaining stock in medium saucepan with reserved marinade,
   bring to a boil. Reduce heat; simmer, stir in cornflour mixture. Cook,
   stirring, about 5 minutes or until sauce boils and thickens.

5 Serve chicken on rice; drizzle with sauce.

SERVES 4

per serving 10.3g fat; 1665kJ
serving suggestion Serve with stir-fried Asian greens.
tip Use only the lower white part of each stem of lemon grass.

honey-mustard chicken with potato kumara mash

PREPARATION TIME 15 MINUTES (plus refrigeration time)
COOKING TIME 15 MINUTES

Soak eight bamboo skewers in water for at least an hour before use to prevent them from splintering and/or scorching. The honey-mustard marinade is also used to make the sauce in this recipe.

8 chicken tenderloins (600g)
1/3 cup (115g) honey
2 tablespoons seeded mustard
1/3 cup (80ml) white vinegar
2 tablespoons soy sauce
3 medium potatoes (600g)
1 small kumara (250g)
2 cloves garlic, sliced thinly
1/4 cup (60ml) skim milk
2 teaspoons fresh thyme leaves

1 Thread each piece of chicken onto a bamboo skewer; place in shallow baking dish. Pour half of the combined honey, mustard, vinegar and sauce over chicken, cover; refrigerate 3 hours or overnight.

2 Preheat oven to hot.

3 Roast undrained chicken, uncovered, in hot oven about 10 minutes or until cooked through.

4 Meanwhile, boil, steam or microwave combined potato, kumara and garlic until tender; drain. Mash in medium bowl with milk; stir in thyme. Heat remaining marinade in small saucepan.

5 Serve chicken with potato kumara mash; drizzle with marinade.

SERVES 4

per serving 8.7g fat; 1842kJ
serving suggestion Serve with steamed green vegetables or a green salad.
tips You can grill or barbecue the chicken rather than bake it.
Lightly oil the tablespoon to make the honey easier to measure.

crumbed fish with warm tomato salad

PREPARATION TIME 15 MINUTES • COOKING TIME 25 MINUTES

You can use flathead, snapper, ling, bream or any other firm white fish in this recipe.

cooking-oil spray
1 medium red onion (170g)
250g cherry tomatoes
1/4 cup (60ml) white wine vinegar
2 cloves garlic, crushed
1/3 cup (55g) corn flake crumbs
1 teaspoon ground cumin
1 teaspoon sweet paprika
1 teaspoon ground turmeric
4 firm white fish fillets (720g)
1/4 cup (35g) plain flour
2 egg whites, beaten lightly
150g baby spinach leaves
1/4 cup (50g) drained capers

1 Preheat oven to hot.

2 Spray oven tray lightly with cooking-oil spray. Cut onion into thin wedges. Place onion and tomatoes on tray; drizzle with combined vinegar and garlic. Roast, uncovered, about 20 minutes or until tomatoes are softened.

3 Combine crumbs and spices in small bowl.

4 Meanwhile, coat fish in flour; shake away excess. Dip fish in egg white, coat in crumb mixture. Spray fish both sides with cooking-oil spray; cook, uncovered, in heated large non-stick frying pan until browned both sides and cooked through.

5 Combine spinach and capers in large bowl with tomato and onion mixture; serve with fish.

SERVES 4

per serving 5.6g fat; 1327kJ

tip Fish can be coated in crumb mixture 2 hours before cooking time; store, covered, in refrigerator.

tuna and asparagus frittata

PREPARATION TIME 10 MINUTES • COOKING TIME 30 MINUTES

A frittata, Italian in origin, is a type of omelette cooked either in a frying pan, on top of the stove, or in the oven until set through. It makes great picnic fare or a welcome addition to the antipasto plate.

**5 medium potatoes (1kg),
   sliced thinly**
**1 medium brown onion (150g),
   sliced thinly**
1 clove garlic, crushed
**250g asparagus, trimmed,
   chopped coarsely**
**425g can tuna in spring
   water, drained**
4 eggs, beaten lightly
4 egg whites, beaten lightly
**2 tablespoons finely chopped
   fresh flat-leaf parsley**
cooking-oil spray

1 Boil, steam or microwave potato until almost tender.

2 Cook onion and garlic in heated small non-stick frying pan, stirring, until onion softens.

3 Combine potato and onion mixture in large bowl with asparagus, tuna, egg, egg white and parsley.

4 Reheat same pan; spray lightly with cooking-oil spray. Spoon frittata mixture into pan, press down firmly; cook, uncovered, over low heat until almost set. Remove from heat; place under heated grill until frittata sets and top is browned lightly.

SERVES 4

per serving 8.2g fat; 1496kJ

serving suggestion Serve with a salad of baby rocket leaves drizzled with balsamic vinegar.

tip Substitute well-drained canned asparagus for the fresh, if desired.

salmon and roast potato salad

PREPARATION TIME 10 MINUTES • COOKING TIME 30 MINUTES (plus cooling time)

**500g kipfler potatoes,
chopped coarsely**
425g can pink salmon
**2 medium tomatoes (380g),
cut into wedges**
1 baby cos lettuce, torn roughly
1/2 cup (120g) sour cream
**1 medium red onion (170g),
chopped finely**
**1/4 cup (50g) drained capers,
chopped finely**
**2 tablespoons finely chopped
fresh dill**
2 tablespoons lemon juice

1 Preheat oven to hot.

2 Place potato in large lightly oiled baking dish; roast, uncovered, stirring occasionally, in hot oven about 30 minutes or until browned and crisp. Allow potato to cool.

3 Drain salmon; remove any bones and skin, then flake with fork in large serving bowl.

4 Place cooled potato in bowl with salmon; add tomato and lettuce, toss to combine. Drizzle with combined remaining ingredients just before serving.

SERVES 4

per serving 17.6g fat; 1437kJ

greek barbecued octopus salad

PREPARATION TIME 10 MINUTES (plus refrigeration time)
COOKING TIME 10 MINUTES (plus cooling time)

Capture the essence of an Aegean summer with this flavour-packed Greek-style salad.

1/3 cup (80ml) lemon juice
1 tablespoon honey
4 cloves garlic, crushed
1/4 teaspoon cayenne pepper
1kg cleaned baby octopus, halved
100g baby spinach leaves
1 small red onion (100g), sliced thinly
250g cherry tomatoes, halved
1 tablespoon finely shredded fresh mint leaves
1 tablespoon finely shredded fresh basil leaves
100g fetta cheese, chopped coarsely

1 Combine juice, honey, garlic, pepper and octopus in large bowl, cover; refrigerate 3 hours or overnight.

2 Drain octopus over large bowl; reserve marinade. Cook octopus, in batches, on heated oiled grill plate (or barbecue or grill) until tender.

3 Meanwhile, place reserved marinade in small saucepan; bring to a boil. Reduce heat; simmer, uncovered, about 5 minutes or until marinade reduces slightly, cool.

4 Just before serving, place octopus and marinade in large bowl with remaining ingredients; toss gently to combine.

SERVES 4

per serving 8.6g fat; 1278kJ

serving suggestion Serve with a bowl of tzatziki, that piquant Greek combination of cucumber, yogurt and garlic.

tip You could substitute rocket or any other salad green for the spinach.

fruit nibble mix

PREPARATION TIME 10 MINUTES
COOKING TIME 5 MINUTES

3 puffed corn cakes (35g), crumbled
1/2 cup (10g) puffed wheat
1/2 teaspoon sesame oil
2 teaspoons teriyaki sauce
1 tablespoon honey
12 grissini (30g)
1/4 cup (35g) dried apricots, halved
1/4 cup (20g) dried apples, halved
1/4 cup (40g) dried dates, pitted,
**   chopped coarsely**
1/4 cup (40g) sultanas

1 Preheat oven to hot. Combine corn
   cake, puffed wheat, oil, sauce and
   honey in medium bowl; spread mixture
   in even layer on oven tray. Roast,
   uncovered, in hot oven about
   5 minutes or until just crisp and
   toasted, stirring occasionally.

2 Break grissini into small pieces; place
   in large bowl with cooled corn cake
   mixture and remaining ingredients.
   Toss gently to combine.

SERVES 4

per serving   1.8g fat; 773kJ

mustard munch

PREPARATION TIME 10 MINUTES
COOKING TIME 20 MINUTES

4 puffed rice cakes (50g)
50g sesame rice crackers
1 cup (20g) puffed wheat
1 cup (20g) puffed rice
1 egg white, beaten lightly
2 teaspoons salt
1 teaspoon ground turmeric
2 teaspoons sweet paprika
2 teaspoons mustard powder
1 tablespoon seeded mustard

1 Preheat oven to moderately slow. Break
   rice cakes and rice crackers into pieces.

2 Combine rice cake, crackers, puffed
   wheat and puffed rice in bowl; stir in
   egg white, salt, spices and mustard.

3 Spread mixture onto lightly oiled oven
   tray; roast, uncovered, in moderately
   slow oven about 20 minutes or until
   mustard munch is crisp.

SERVES 4

per serving   2.4g fat; 633kJ

Above: fruit nibble mix.
Opposite: mustard munch (back); indian popcorn (front).

nibbles

Satisfy the munchies and keep a clear conscience about your health with this crunchy collection.

indian popcorn

PREPARATION TIME 5 MINUTES
COOKING TIME 20 MINUTES

¹/₂ cup (115g) popping corn
100g mixed spiced pappadums
2 teaspoons ground cumin
2 teaspoons ground coriander
1 teaspoon ground cinnamon

1 Place popping corn in an oven bag or paper bag; secure bag loosely with kitchen string. Place bag on microwave oven turntable; cook on MEDIUM-HIGH (70%) for about 4 minutes or until popped. Remove bag from microwave oven with tongs; stand for 2 minutes before opening bag.

2 Microwave pappadums, uncovered, on HIGH (100%) about 30 seconds or until puffed. Break roughly into small pieces.

3 Cook combined spices in small dry heated frying pan until fragrant.

4 Place popcorn and pappadum in large bowl with spice mixture; toss gently to combine.

MAKES 12 CUPS (195g)

per ¹/₂ cup serving 0.4g fat; 132kJ

mains

These grills, bakes, pastas, curries and stir-fries come complete with accompaniments, for ease of planning and preparation, and for keeping track of fat and kilojoule counts.

satay beef stir-fry with hokkien noodles

PREPARATION TIME 15 MINUTES • COOKING TIME 15 MINUTES

Ketjap manis, a thick sweet soy sauce of Indonesian origin, is available at many supermarkets and Asian food stores.

600g hokkien noodles
300g beef rump steak,
  sliced thinly
1/2 teaspoon finely grated
  fresh ginger
2 teaspoons sesame oil
1 small red onion (100g),
  sliced thinly
1 medium red capsicum (200g),
  sliced thinly
150g broccoli florets
2 teaspoons lime juice
1/4 cup (60ml) satay sauce
1 tablespoon hoisin sauce
1/3 cup (80ml) soy sauce
1 tablespoon ketjap manis
150g snow peas
1 tablespoon finely chopped
  fresh coriander leaves
1/4 cup (35g) unsalted roasted
  peanuts, chopped coarsely

1 Rinse noodles under hot water; drain. Transfer to large bowl; separate noodles with fork.

2 Heat oiled wok or large non-stick frying pan; stir-fry beef and ginger, in batches, until browned.

3 Heat oil in same wok; stir-fry onion, capsicum and broccoli until just tender. Return beef to wok with combined juice and sauces; stir-fry until sauce boils. Add noodles and snow peas; stir-fry until hot.

4 Add coriander; stir-fry until combined. Serve sprinkled with peanuts.

SERVES 4

per serving 15.8g fat; 2788kJ

serving suggestion Serve with a bowl of sambal oelek, the fiery-hot Indonesian chilli and vinegar sauce.

veal with potato pea mash

PREPARATION TIME 10 MINUTES • COOKING TIME 20 MINUTES

There's not a hint of deprivation in this satisfying combination of veal and mash.

450g veal steaks
1/3 cup (50g) plain flour
1 egg white, beaten lightly
2 tablespoons skim milk
1 cup (160g) corn flake crumbs
1 teaspoon finely grated
** lemon rind**
2 tablespoons finely chopped
** fresh flat-leaf parsley**
cooking-oil spray
4 medium potatoes (800g)
1/4 cup (60ml) buttermilk
3/4 cup (180ml) chicken stock
2 cups (250g) frozen peas
1 lemon, cut into 8 wedges

1 Preheat oven to very hot.

2 Cut each steak in half. Toss veal in flour; shake away excess flour. Coat veal in combined egg white and milk, then in combined crumbs, rind and parsley.

3 Place veal in single layer on lightly oiled oven tray; spray lightly with cooking-oil spray. Bake veal, uncovered, in very hot oven about 5 minutes or until cooked through. Stand 5 minutes, slice thickly.

4 Meanwhile, boil, steam or microwave potatoes until soft; drain. Mash potatoes with buttermilk in medium bowl; cover to keep warm.

5 Place stock in medium saucepan; bring to a boil. Add peas; cook, uncovered, until stock reduces by half. Blend or process until pea mixture is almost pureed.

6 Gently swirl pea mixture into potato mash to give marbled effect. Divide potato and pea mash among plates; top with veal. Serve with lemon.

SERVES 4

per serving 4.3g fat; 2154kJ

serving suggestion Serve with a contrasting coloured vegetable such as boiled or steamed carrots, corn on the cob, or oven-roasted tomatoes.

tip Veal can be crumbed several hours ahead; store, covered, in refrigerator.

pork with ratatouille and potatoes

PREPARATION TIME 10 MINUTES • COOKING TIME 25 MINUTES

In a Provençale dialect, touiller means to stir and crush, thus the name ratatouille perfectly describes this rich vegetable stew.

1kg tiny new potatoes, halved
1 medium brown onion (150g), chopped coarsely
2 cloves garlic, crushed
4 baby eggplants (240g), chopped coarsely
2 medium green zucchini (240g), chopped coarsely
400g can tomatoes
2 tablespoons finely shredded fresh basil leaves
4 x 150g pork steaks

1 Preheat oven to very hot.

2 Place potato in large lightly oiled baking dish; roast, uncovered, in very hot oven about 25 minutes or until browned and crisp.

3 Meanwhile, cook onion and garlic in heated large non-stick frying pan, stirring, until onion softens. Stir in eggplant and zucchini; cook, stirring, until vegetables are just tender.

4 Stir in undrained crushed tomatoes; bring to a boil. Reduce heat; simmer, uncovered, about 5 minutes or until vegetables are tender and sauce thickens. Stir in basil.

5 Cook pork, in batches, in heated medium non-stick frying pan until browned both sides and cooked as desired. Slice pork thickly.

6 Serve pork with potatoes and ratatouille.

SERVES 4

per serving 6.2g fat; 1652kJ
serving suggestion A green salad goes well with this dish.
tip Ratatouille can be made a day ahead; store, covered, in refrigerator. It is great on its own, or served with pasta.

pork fillet with apple and leek

PREPARATION TIME 10 MINUTES • COOKING TIME 25 MINUTES

Pork has a natural affinity with both apple and onion; here, these traditional accompaniments are given a contemporary twist.

800g pork fillets
3/4 cup (180ml) chicken stock
2 medium leeks (700g),
    sliced thickly
1 clove garlic, crushed
2 tablespoons brown sugar
2 tablespoons red wine vinegar
2 medium apples (300g)
10g butter
1 tablespoon brown sugar, extra
400g baby carrots,
    trimmed, halved
8 medium patty-pan squash
    (100g), quartered
250g asparagus, trimmed,
    coarsely chopped

1 Preheat oven to very hot.

2 Place pork, in single layer, in large baking dish; bake, uncovered, in very hot oven about 25 minutes or until pork is browned and cooked as desired. Cover; stand 5 minutes before slicing thickly.

3 Meanwhile, heat half of the stock in medium frying pan; cook leek and garlic, stirring, until leek softens and browns slightly. Add sugar and vinegar; cook, stirring, about 5 minutes or until leek caramelises. Add remaining stock; bring to a boil. Reduce heat; simmer, uncovered, about 5 minutes or until liquid reduces by half. Place leek mixture in medium bowl; cover to keep warm.

4 Peel, core and halve apples; cut into thick slices.

5 Melt butter in same pan; cook apple and extra sugar, stirring, until apple is browned and tender.

6 Boil, steam or microwave carrot, squash and asparagus, separately, until just tender; drain.

7 Serve pork, topped with caramelised apple and sweet and sour leek, on top of the mixed vegetables.

SERVES 4

per serving 7.5g fat; 1624kJ

serving suggestion Potatoes – boiled, mashed or baked – would make a good accompaniment for this dish.

tip You can make the sweet and sour leek several hours ahead; just reheat before serving.

warm lamb salad with croutons

PREPARATION TIME 10 MINUTES • COOKING TIME 15 MINUTES

Crouton comes from the French word croûte, which translates as crust – hence these crunchy pieces of garlic bread that soak up the sauce in this dish.

4 slices white bread
1 tablespoon vegetable oil
1 clove garlic, crushed
4 medium zucchini (480g),
**   sliced thinly**
4 baby eggplants (240g),
**   sliced thinly**
8 lamb cutlets (600g)
¹/₂ cup (125ml) balsamic vinegar
¹/₂ cup (125ml) beef stock
150g curly endive
3 medium tomatoes (570g),
**   chopped coarsely**
¹/₄ cup loosely packed, coarsely
**   chopped fresh flat-leaf parsley**

1 Preheat oven to hot.

2 Trim crusts from bread; discard crusts. Halve each slice diagonally; combine with oil and garlic in small bowl, mix well. Place bread in single layer on oven tray; toast, uncovered, turning once, in hot oven about 4 minutes each side or until croutons are browned lightly and crisp.

3 Cook zucchini and eggplant, in batches, in heated large non-stick frying pan until just tender; cover to keep warm. Cook lamb, in batches, in same pan until browned both sides and cooked as desired; cover to keep warm.

4 Place vinegar in same pan; bring to a boil. Add stock; reduce heat. Simmer, uncovered, until sauce reduces by half.

5 Serve lamb on croutons with combined zucchini, eggplant, endive, tomato and parsley. Drizzle with balsamic dressing.

SERVES 4

per serving 13.2g fat; 1244kJ

tip Croutons can be made a day ahead and stored in an airtight container.

chickpea and pumpkin curry

PREPARATION TIME 10 MINUTES • COOKING TIME 25 MINUTES

In Indian cooking, the word masala loosely translates as paste; the word tikka refers to a bite-sized piece of meat, poultry, fish or vegetable. A jar labelled tikka masala contains spices and oils, mixed to a mild paste.

2 teaspoons peanut oil
2 medium brown onions (300g),
** sliced thinly**
2 cloves garlic, crushed
2 tablespoons tikka masala
** curry paste**
2 cups (500ml) vegetable stock
1 cup (250ml) water
1kg butternut pumpkin,
** chopped coarsely**
2 cups (400g) jasmine rice
300g can chickpeas,
** rinsed, drained**
1 cup (125g) frozen peas
1/4 cup (60ml) low-fat cream
2 tablespoons chopped fresh
** coriander leaves**

1 Heat oil in large saucepan; cook onion and garlic, stirring, until onion softens. Add paste; cook, stirring, until fragrant. Stir in stock and the water; bring to a boil. Add pumpkin; reduce heat. Simmer, covered, 15 minutes or until pumpkin is almost tender.

2 Meanwhile, cook rice in large saucepan of boiling water, uncovered, until tender; drain. Cover to keep warm.

3 Add chickpeas and peas to curry; cook, stirring, until hot. Stir in cream and coriander. Serve curry with rice.

SERVES 4

per serving 12.5g fat; 2631kJ

serving suggestion Serve with a fresh tomato sambal, pickles or chutney, and pappadums puffed in the microwave oven.

tip Make the curry a day ahead to allow the flavours to develop better.

lamb chermoulla with chickpea salad

PREPARATION TIME 15 MINUTES • COOKING TIME 15 MINUTES

Chermoulla is a Moroccan mixture of fresh and ground spices including coriander, cumin and paprika. It can be used as a marinade for chicken, meat and fish.

300g green beans, trimmed
2 teaspoons cracked black pepper
2 teaspoons ground cumin
2 teaspoons ground coriander
1 teaspoon hot paprika
2 tablespoons coarsely chopped fresh flat-leaf parsley
2 tablespoons coarsely chopped fresh coriander leaves
2 tablespoons coarsely chopped fresh mint leaves
1 tablespoon coarsely grated lemon rind
1/4 cup (60ml) water
1 medium red onion (170g), chopped finely
8 lamb fillets (700g)
400g can brown lentils, rinsed, drained
300g can chickpeas, rinsed, drained
1/3 cup loosely packed, coarsely chopped
**   fresh flat-leaf parsley, extra**
2 cloves garlic, crushed
2 tablespoons lemon juice

1   Cut beans into 3cm lengths; boil, steam or microwave beans until just tender. Refresh under cold water; drain.

2   Blend or process pepper, spices, herbs, rind, the water and half of the onion until mixture forms a paste.

3   Coat lamb with chermoulla paste in large bowl; cook, in batches, on heated oiled grill plate (or grill or barbecue) until browned and cooked as desired. Cover; stand 5 minutes before slicing thickly.

4   Combine beans, lentils, chickpeas, extra parsley, garlic and juice with remaining onion in large bowl; toss gently to combine. Serve chickpea salad with lamb.

SERVES 4

per serving 8.3g fat; 1373kJ

serving suggestion Serve with a bowl of minted yogurt.

tip The salad can be assembled several hours ahead; add juice just before serving.

fettuccine bolognese

PREPARATION TIME 5 MINUTES • COOKING TIME 25 MINUTES

1 small brown onion (80g),
chopped finely
2 cloves garlic, crushed
1 small carrot (70g),
chopped finely
1 trimmed stick celery (75g),
chopped finely
400g lean minced beef
2 cups (500ml) bottled tomato
pasta sauce
1/2 cup (125ml) beef stock
375g fettuccine

1 Cook onion and garlic in heated large non-stick frying pan, stirring, until onion softens. Add carrot and celery; cook, stirring, until vegetables are just tender.

2 Add beef; cook, stirring, until changed in colour. Add sauce and stock; bring to a boil. Reduce heat; simmer, uncovered, about 15 minutes or until mixture thickens slightly.

3 Meanwhile, cook pasta in large saucepan of boiling water, uncovered, until just tender; drain.

4 Serve fettuccine topped with bolognese sauce.

SERVES 4

per serving 10.2g fat; 2361kJ

serving suggestion Serve with a green salad and a loaf of ciabatta.

tip The flavour of the bolognese will improve if it is made a day ahead; reheat just before serving.

steak bourguignon with celeriac-potato mash

PREPARATION TIME 10 MINUTES • COOKING TIME 20 MINUTES

You can substitute rib-eye (scotch fillet) or sirloin (New York cut) steak for the eye fillet in this recipe.

**1 small celeriac (600g),
  chopped coarsely**
**2 medium potatoes (400g),
  chopped coarsely**
1/4 cup (60ml) skim milk
20g butter
4 x 200g beef eye-fillet steaks
200g button mushrooms, halved
6 baby onions (150g), quartered
2 cloves garlic, crushed
1/2 cup (125ml) dry red wine
1 cup (250ml) beef stock
1 tablespoon tomato paste
2 teaspoons cornflour
2 teaspoons water
**1 tablespoon coarsely chopped
  fresh oregano**

1 Boil, steam or microwave celeriac and potato, separately, until tender; drain. Mash in medium bowl with milk and butter, cover to keep warm.

2 Meanwhile, cook beef in heated large non-stick frying pan until browned both sides and cooked as desired; cover to keep warm.

3 Cook mushrooms, onion and garlic in same pan until vegetables just soften. Add wine, stock and paste; simmer, uncovered, about 5 minutes. Stir in blended cornflour and water; cook, stirring, until sauce boils and thickens.

4 Serve beef with mash and bourguignon sauce; sprinkle with oregano.

SERVES 4

per serving 14.3g fat; 1855kJ

serving suggestion Serve with steamed greens such as asparagus or broccoli.

tip Mash can be made a day ahead and kept, covered, in refrigerator; reheat just before serving. Incidentally, mash responds well to being reheated in a microwave oven.

gnocchi with herb and mushroom sauce

PREPARATION TIME 10 MINUTES • COOKING TIME 15 MINUTES

Gnocchi are small dumplings made of such ingredients as flour, potatoes, semolina, ricotta cheese or spinach. They make a great base for a full-flavoured sauce such as this, packed with herbs, red wine and mushrooms.

1 tablespoon vegetable oil
1 medium brown onion (150g), chopped coarsely
2 cloves garlic, crushed
400g swiss brown mushrooms, sliced thinly
1 tablespoon plain flour
1/3 cup (80ml) dry red wine
2 teaspoons soy sauce
2/3 cup (160ml) vegetable stock
1 tablespoon light sour cream
1 tablespoon coarsely chopped fresh oregano
1 tablespoon finely chopped fresh sage
600g fresh potato gnocchi

1 Heat oil in large frying pan; cook onion, garlic and mushrooms, stirring, until vegetables are just tender. Add flour; cook, stirring, 1 minute.

2 Add wine, sauce, stock and cream; cook, stirring, until sauce thickens slightly. Stir in herbs.

3 Meanwhile, cook gnocchi in large saucepan of boiling water, uncovered, until gnocchi rise to the surface and are just tender; drain. Add gnocchi to herb and mushroom sauce; toss gently to combine.

SERVES 4

per serving 7.6g fat; 1397kJ

serving suggestion Serve with a green salad, dressed with herb vinaigrette, and fresh crusty bread.

tip You could substitute button or oyster mushrooms for the swiss brown.

mustard veal with polenta and spinach puree

PREPARATION TIME 15 MINUTES • COOKING TIME 20 MINUTES

Polenta is the Italian answer to mashed potato – the perfect accompaniment for soaking up meat juices and too-good-to-waste sauces.

1/3 cup (95g) seeded mustard
2 tablespoons coarsely chopped fresh oregano
2 cloves garlic, crushed
4 veal chops (600g)
4 large egg tomatoes (360g), halved
2 cups (500ml) water
1 teaspoon salt
1 cup (170g) polenta
3/4 cup (180ml) skim milk
1/4 cup (20g) finely grated parmesan cheese
2kg spinach, trimmed
2 cloves garlic, crushed, extra
2 anchovy fillets, drained
2 tablespoons lemon juice
1/4 cup (60ml) beef stock

1 Combine mustard, oregano and garlic in small bowl; brush veal both sides with mustard mixture.

2 Cook veal and tomato, in batches, on heated lightly oiled grill plate (or grill or barbecue) until veal is browned both sides and cooked as desired and tomato is browned and tender.

3 Meanwhile, bring combined water and salt to a boil in medium saucepan. Stir in polenta; cook, stirring, about 10 minutes or until polenta thickens. Stir in milk; cook, stirring, about 5 minutes or until polenta thickens. Stir in cheese.

4 Boil, steam or microwave spinach until just wilted; squeeze out excess liquid with hands. Blend or process spinach with remaining ingredients until pureed.

5 Serve veal chops with tomato, polenta and pureed spinach.

SERVES 4

per serving 7.3g fat; 1626kJ

serving suggestion Top steaks with fresh sage leaves, and serve with a radicchio or rocket salad dressed in balsamic vinegar.

tip Fresh rosemary or thyme can be substituted for the oregano.

beef steak with capsicum relish

PREPARATION TIME 10 MINUTES • COOKING TIME 20 MINUTES

You can substitute rib-eye (scotch fillet) or sirloin (New York cut) steak for the eye fillet in this recipe.

3 medium red capsicums (600g)
1 teaspoon olive oil
1 large brown onion (200g),
sliced thinly
2 cloves garlic, sliced thinly
2 tablespoons brown sugar
2 tablespoons sherry vinegar
3 red thai chillies, seeded,
chopped finely
4 x 200g beef eye fillet steaks
2 corn cobs (800g), trimmed,
chopped coarsely
150g sugar snap peas
300g tiny new potatoes, halved
2 tablespoons finely chopped
fresh flat-leaf parsley

1 Quarter capsicums; remove and discard seeds and membranes. Roast under grill or in very hot oven, skin-side up, until skin blisters and blackens. Cover with plastic or paper for 5 minutes; peel away skin, slice thinly.

2 Heat oil in medium frying pan; cook onion and garlic, stirring, until soft. Add sugar, vinegar, chilli and capsicum; cook, stirring, 5 minutes.

3 Meanwhile, cook beef on heated oiled grill plate (or grill or barbecue) until browned and cooked as desired.

4 Boil, steam or microwave vegetables, separately, until just tender; drain.

5 Top steaks with capsicum relish; serve with vegetables, sprinkle with parsley.

SERVES 4

per serving 13g fat; 2327kJ

serving suggestion Serve with a green salad with vinaigrette.

tip You can make the capsicum relish a day ahead; store, covered, in refrigerator. Reheat just before serving.

cauliflower vegetable curry

PREPARATION TIME 10 MINUTES • COOKING TIME 20 MINUTES

Contrasting colours add eye appeal to this fragrant curry, which would traditionally be served with naan or puri in Indian homes. You can substitute equivalent weights of peas, capsicum, mushrooms or zucchini if you prefer them to the vegetables suggested in the recipe.

1 medium brown onion (150g), sliced thickly
2 red thai chillies, chopped coarsely
1 clove garlic, crushed
2 tablespoons mild curry paste
4 small potatoes (480g), chopped coarsely
500g cauliflower florets
1¹/₂ cups (375ml) vegetable stock
1¹/₂ cups (375ml) water
2 cups (400g) jasmine rice
200g green beans, halved
400ml light coconut milk
4 hard-boiled eggs, sliced thickly
¹/₄ cup loosely packed fresh coriander leaves

1 Cook onion, chilli and garlic in heated large non-stick saucepan, stirring, until onion softens. Stir in paste; cook, stirring, until fragrant. Add potato and cauliflower; cook, stirring, until coated in curry mixture. Add stock and the water; bring to a boil. Reduce heat; simmer, covered, about 10 minutes or until potato is just tender.

2 Meanwhile, cook rice in large saucepan of boiling water, uncovered, until just tender; drain. Cover to keep warm.

3 Stir beans into curry mixture; cook, uncovered, until just tender. Stir in coconut milk and egg; simmer, uncovered, until hot. Serve curry with rice; sprinkle with coriander.

SERVES 4

per serving 16.6g fat; 2837kJ

serving suggestion Serve with raita made with low-fat yogurt and cucumber, and pappadums cooked in the microwave oven.

tandoori lamb with cucumber raita

PREPARATION TIME 10 MINUTES • COOKING TIME 20 MINUTES

8 lamb fillets (700g)
1 tablespoon tandoori paste
400g low-fat yogurt
1 lebanese cucumber (130g),
 seeded, chopped finely
2 green onions, chopped finely
1/2 teaspoon ground cumin
1 teaspoon ground cardamom
2 cups (400g) basmati rice
pinch saffron threads

1 Combine lamb with paste and half of the yogurt in large bowl. Combine remaining yogurt in small bowl with cucumber, onion and half of the combined spices.

2 Place rice and saffron in large saucepan of boiling water; cook, uncovered, until rice is tender. Drain rice; place in large bowl.

3 Toast remaining spices in heated dry small frying pan until fragrant; stir into saffron rice, cover to keep warm.

4 Cook undrained lamb, in batches, on heated lightly oiled grill plate (or grill or barbecue) until browned and cooked as desired.

5 Serve lamb on saffron rice, topped with cucumber raita.

SERVES 4

per serving 8.6g fat; 1869kJ

serving suggestion Serve with a fresh tomato and onion sambal, and pappadums cooked in the microwave oven.

tip You can marinate the lamb a day ahead; store, covered, in refrigerator. Similarly, the cucumber raita can be made several hours ahead; store, covered, in refrigerator.

vegetable and tofu stir-fry

PREPARATION TIME 10 MINUTES • COOKING TIME 15 MINUTES

*Tofu, also known as bean curd, is made from the "milk" of crushed soy beans.
Its fairly mild flavour is enhanced by the vegetables and sauce.*

250g fresh firm tofu
250g fresh rice noodles
1 tablespoon peanut oil
1 large brown onion (200g),
   sliced thickly
2 cloves garlic, crushed
1 teaspoon five-spice powder
300g button mushrooms, halved
200g swiss brown
   mushrooms, halved
1/4 cup (60ml) soy sauce
1 cup (250ml) vegetable stock
1/4 cup (60ml) water
300g baby bok choy,
   chopped coarsely
300g choy sum, chopped coarsely
4 green onions, chopped coarsely
200g bean sprouts

1 Cut tofu into 2cm cubes. Rinse noodles under hot water; drain. Transfer to large bowl; separate noodles with fork.

2 Heat oil in wok or large frying pan; stir-fry brown onion and garlic until onion softens. Add five-spice; stir-fry until fragrant. Add mushrooms; stir-fry until almost tender.

3 Add combined sauce, stock and the water; bring to a boil. Add bok choy, choy sum and green onion; stir-fry until bok choy just wilts. Add tofu, noodles and sprouts; stir-fry until hot.

SERVES 4

per serving 9.3g fat; 1321kJ

tip You can use rice stick noodles if fresh noodles are not available. Place rice stick noodles in a large heatproof bowl; cover with boiling water. Stand until just tender then drain.

spaghetti with tomato and white beans

PREPARATION TIME 10 MINUTES • COOKING TIME 20 MINUTES

Beans are an Italian staple and are often served with spaghetti, that other great favourite, in the same dish.

1/3 cup (80ml) vegetable stock
1 small red onion (100g),
   chopped finely
2 cloves garlic, crushed
1 cup (250ml) dry white wine
1/2 teaspoon sugar
2 cups (500ml) bottled tomato
   pasta sauce
375g spaghetti
1 tablespoon coarsely chopped
   fresh oregano
2 tablespoons drained capers,
   chopped coarsely
1/2 cup (60g) seeded black
   olives, quartered
300g can butter beans,
   rinsed, drained
2 tablespoons coarsely chopped
   fresh flat-leaf parsley

1 Heat half of the stock in medium saucepan; cook onion and garlic, stirring, until onion softens. Stir in wine, remaining stock, sugar and sauce; bring to a boil. Reduce heat; simmer, uncovered, until sauce thickens slightly.

2 Cook pasta in large saucepan of boiling water, uncovered, until just tender; drain.

3 Meanwhile, stir remaining ingredients into sauce; cook, stirring, until hot. Serve spaghetti with tomato and white bean sauce.

SERVES 4

per serving 2.4g fat; 1938kJ
serving suggestion If you are not overly concerned about fat counts, serve with parmesan.
tip Make sauce a day ahead; store, covered, in refrigerator.

asian-style fish

PREPARATION TIME 10 MINUTES • COOKING TIME 20 MINUTES

You can use any small, whole white-fleshed fish for this recipe. Baby barramundi or snapper would make excellent substitutes for the bream.

4 x 350g bream
6 green onions, sliced thinly
50g fresh ginger, sliced thinly
4 cloves garlic, sliced thinly
2 tablespoons soy sauce
2 tablespoons dry sherry
2 tablespoons brown sugar
1/3 cup (80ml) vegetable stock
500g choy sum, chopped coarsely
500g chinese broccoli, chopped coarsely

1 Preheat oven to moderately hot. Score each fish three times both sides; place on individual pieces of foil big enough to wrap fish.

2 Combine onion, ginger, garlic, sauce, sherry, sugar and stock in small bowl; divide mixture over each fish. Wrap fish securely in foil; place on oven tray in single layer. Bake in moderately hot oven about 20 minutes or until fish are cooked through.

3 Meanwhile, boil, steam or microwave choy sum and broccoli, separately, until just wilted; drain.

4 Transfer fish and onion-and-ginger mixture to serving plates. Serve with vegetables.

SERVES 4

per serving 10.2g fat; 1331kJ

serving suggestion Serve with steamed or boiled white rice and a bowl of combined ketjap manis and chopped chilli.

tip Fish can be assembled and wrapped in foil several hours ahead; ensure against the sauce leaking out by using a double layer of foil. Store fish parcels in refrigerator until cooking time.

phad thai

PREPARATION TIME 15 MINUTES • COOKING TIME 15 MINUTES

Noodles are a favourite Thai snack, and for this dish they usually use sen lek, a 5mm-wide rice stick noodle.

250g rice stick noodles
450g chicken thigh fillets, sliced thinly
1 clove garlic, crushed
1 teaspoon grated fresh ginger
2 red thai chillies, sliced thinly
2 tablespoons chopped palm sugar
2 tablespoons soy sauce
1/4 cup (60ml) sweet chilli sauce
1 tablespoon fish sauce
1 tablespoon lime juice
3 green onions, sliced thinly
1 cup (80g) bean sprouts
1 cup (80g) snow pea sprouts
1/4 cup loosely packed, coarsely chopped
   fresh coriander leaves

1 Place noodles in large heatproof bowl; cover with boiling water. Stand until just tender; drain.

2 Heat wok or large non-stick frying pan; stir-fry chicken, garlic, ginger and chilli, in batches, until chicken is browned.

3 Return chicken mixture to wok with sugar, sauces and juice; stir-fry until sauce thickens slightly. Add noodles, onion and sprouts to wok; stir-fry until hot. Serve phad thai sprinkled with coriander.

SERVES 4

per serving 9.2g fat; 1717kJ

serving suggestion Although this dish is a complete meal in a bowl, the Thais usually accompany it with a soup such as tom yum goong (prawn soup) which is consumed like a beverage throughout the meal.

tips Remove seeds from chilli if you prefer a milder flavour.

Palm sugar, also sold as jaggery, is a product of the coconut palm. Substitute black or brown sugar if you can't find it at your supermarket.

chicken kibbeh burger

PREPARATION TIME 15 MINUTES (plus standing time) • COOKING TIME 10 MINUTES

This recipe combines favourite Middle-Eastern flavours in the chicken patties.
Burghul is made from steamed, dried and crushed wheat kernels.

1/3 cup (55g) burghul
500g chicken mince
1/3 cup loosely packed, coarsely
    chopped fresh flat-leaf parsley
1 small red onion (100g),
    chopped finely
2 teaspoons finely grated
    lemon rind
1 tablespoon lemon juice
1 egg white, beaten lightly
4 wholemeal pocket pitta
2 medium tomatoes (380g),
    sliced thickly
8 baby cos lettuce leaves

LEMON MAYONNAISE

1/3 cup (100g) low-fat
    mayonnaise
2 tablespoons lemon juice
1 clove garlic, crushed

1 Place burghul in small bowl; cover with cold water. Stand 10 minutes; drain. Using hands, squeeze out excess water.

2 Using one hand, combine chicken, parsley, onion, rind, juice and egg white in large bowl. Stir in burghul; using one hand, work in burghul to form a smooth paste. Divide chicken mixture into four patties.

3 Heat large non-stick frying pan; cook patties, uncovered, until browned both sides and cooked through.

4 Split pitta pockets; divide tomato, lettuce and patties among pockets. Drizzle with lemon mayonnaise.

lemon mayonnaise Combine ingredients in small bowl.

SERVES 4

per serving 15.1g fat; 2208kJ

serving suggestion You can replace the lemon mayonnaise with a dollop of hummus, if you prefer.

tip Chicken patties can be made in advance and frozen. Lemon mayonnaise can be made a day ahead; store, covered, in refrigerator.

chicken and potato casserole

PREPARATION TIME 15 MINUTES • COOKING TIME 30 MINUTES

1 tablespoon peanut oil
6 baby onions (150g), quartered
2 cloves garlic, crushed
700g chicken thigh fillets,
   chopped coarsely
300g tiny new
   potatoes, quartered
1 large carrot (180g),
   chopped coarsely
1/4 cup (35g) plain flour
1/3 cup (80ml) dry white wine
420g can chicken consomme
500g asparagus, trimmed, halved
2 tablespoons seeded mustard
1 tablespoon finely grated
   lemon rind
1/3 cup loosely packed, coarsely
   chopped fresh flat-leaf parsley

1 Heat oil in large non-stick saucepan; cook onion and garlic, stirring, until onion softens. Add chicken; cook, stirring, about 5 minutes or until chicken is browned and cooked through.

2 Add potato, carrot and flour; cook, stirring, 5 minutes. Add wine and consomme; cook, stirring, until mixture boils and thickens. Simmer, covered, about 10 minutes or until potato is tender.

3 Add asparagus, mustard and rind; bring to a boil. Reduce heat; simmer, covered, until asparagus is just tender. Stir in parsley.

SERVES 4

per serving 17.4g fat; 1746kJ

serving suggestion Serve with a salad of radicchio, and coral and oakleaf lettuce.

tip This recipe is more flavoursome if made a day ahead; store, covered, in refrigerator. Reheat just before serving.

chicken with lentil salsa

PREPARATION TIME 10 MINUTES • COOKING TIME 15 MINUTES

The spices of North Africa give the chicken a flavour-packed jolt in this dish. And, as it can be served hot or cold, this recipe is a good prepare-ahead dish.

2 teaspoons ground cumin
2 teaspoons ground coriander
1 teaspoon ground turmeric
12 chicken tenderloins (900g)
1¹/₂ cups (300g) red lentils
1 clove garlic, crushed
1 red thai chilli, seeded, chopped finely
1 lebanese cucumber (130g), seeded, chopped finely
1 medium red capsicum (200g), chopped finely
¹/₄ cup (60ml) lemon juice
2 teaspoons peanut oil
2 tablespoons coarsely chopped fresh coriander leaves
2 limes, cut into wedges

1 Combine spices in medium bowl with chicken; toss to coat chicken with spices.

2 Cook lentils in large saucepan of boiling water, uncovered, until just tender; drain. Rinse under cold water; drain. Place lentils in large bowl with garlic, chilli, cucumber, capsicum, juice, oil and fresh coriander.

3 Meanwhile, cook chicken on heated lightly oiled grill pan (or grill or barbecue) until browned both sides and cooked through. Add limes to pan; cook until browned both sides. Serve chicken with lentil salsa and lime wedges.

SERVES 4

per serving 16.8g fat; 2314kJ

serving suggestion Serve accompanied with lavash bread as the main course of a summer lunch.

tip You could add 1 teaspoon of harissa to the salad instead of the chilli.

chutney chicken breast with kashmiri pilaf

PREPARATION TIME 5 MINUTES
COOKING TIME 25 MINUTES (plus standing time)

While many Indian dishes involve long, slow cooking, this recipe captures the essence of the cuisine in a quick and easy char-grill.

1 tablespoon vegetable oil
1 small brown onion (80g), chopped finely
1 clove garlic, crushed
1 teaspoon black mustard seeds
1/4 teaspoon ground cardamom
1/2 teaspoon ground cumin
1/2 teaspoon garam masala
1/2 teaspoon ground turmeric
11/2 cups (300g) long-grain white rice
3 cups (750ml) chicken stock
2 tablespoons coarsely chopped fresh coriander leaves
1/3 cup (80g) mango chutney
2 tablespoons water
4 single chicken breast fillets (680g)

1 Heat oil in medium saucepan; cook onion, garlic and mustard seeds, stirring, until onion softens and seeds pop. Add remaining spices; cook, stirring, until fragrant.

2 Add rice; stir to coat in spices. Add stock; bring to a boil. Reduce heat; simmer, uncovered, until rice is just tender. Stir in coriander; keep warm.

3 Meanwhile, combine chutney with the water in small saucepan; cook, stirring, until heated through.

4 Cook chicken, brushing all over with chutney mixture, on heated oiled grill plate (or grill or barbecue) until browned both sides and cooked through. Cut into thick slices. Serve chutney chicken with pilaf.

SERVES 4

per serving 15.3g fat; 2561kJ
serving suggestion Serve with some extra mango chutney and low-fat raita.
tip Mango chutney will burn if the grill or barbecue is too hot.

spicy couscous chicken with fresh corn salsa

PREPARATION TIME 15 MINUTES
COOKING TIME 12 MINUTES (plus standing time)

Couscous, the North African cereal made from semolina, lends an intriguing crunch to the coating on the chicken.

1/2 teaspoon ground cumin
1/4 teaspoon ground coriander
1/4 teaspoon garam masala
1/4 teaspoon ground turmeric
1 cup (250ml) chicken stock
1 cup (200g) couscous
700g single chicken breast fillets
1 egg white, beaten lightly
2 trimmed corn cobs (500g)
2 medium tomatoes (380g), seeded, chopped coarsely
1 small avocado (200g), chopped coarsely
2 tablespoons red wine vinegar
4 green onions, chopped finely

1 Preheat oven to hot.

2 Cook spices in medium heated saucepan, stirring, until fragrant; add stock. Bring to a boil; stir in couscous. Remove from heat; stand, covered, about 5 minutes or until stock is absorbed, fluffing with fork occasionally to separate grains.

3 Mix chicken with egg white; coat in couscous. Place chicken, in single layer, in large lightly oiled baking dish; bake, uncovered, in hot oven about 10 minutes or until chicken is cooked through. Cover to keep warm.

4 Meanwhile, remove kernels from corn cobs. Cook kernels in small pan of boiling water, uncovered, about 2 minutes or until just tender; drain. Rinse under cold water; drain. Combine corn with remaining ingredients in medium bowl. Serve corn salsa with thickly sliced chicken.

SERVES 4

per serving 19.1g fat; 2515kJ

serving suggestion You might like to add some coarsely chopped fresh coriander or finely chopped fresh chilli to the corn salsa. Serve with snow pea sprouts, if desired.

tip The salsa, without the avocado, can be prepared about 3 hours ahead; store, covered, in refrigerator. Add avocado just before serving.

thai fish cakes with noodle salad

PREPARATION TIME 15 MINUTES • COOKING TIME 10 MINUTES

Redfish, usually sold skinned as fillets, is ideal for these fish cakes because of its delicate flavour.
You can, however, use practically any mild-flavoured, skinless fish fillet.

**2/3 cup loosely packed fresh
  coriander leaves**
**1/2 cup loosely packed fresh
  mint leaves**
4 red thai chillies, quartered
**600g firm white fish fillets,
  chopped coarsely**
1 clove garlic, quartered
1 egg white, beaten lightly
250g rice vermicelli
2 teaspoons sugar
1/4 cup (60ml) lime juice
1 tablespoon sambal oelek
**1 lebanese cucumber (130g),
  seeded, chopped finely**
100g snow peas, sliced thinly

1 Blend or process half of the
   coriander, half of the mint, half
   of the chilli, fish, garlic and
   egg white until mixture forms
   a paste; using one hand, shape
   into 12 patties.

2 Cook patties, in batches, in
   heated large non-stick frying
   pan until browned both sides
   and cooked through.

3 Meanwhile, place noodles in
   large heatproof bowl; cover with
   boiling water. Stand until just
   tender; drain. Keep warm.

4 Combine sugar, juice and sambal
   in small saucepan; bring to a
   boil. Reduce heat; simmer,
   stirring, until sugar dissolves.

5 Meanwhile, chop remaining
   coriander, mint and chilli finely.
   Place in large bowl with
   noodles, sugar mixture,
   cucumber and snowpeas;
   toss to combine.

6 Serve fish cakes on noodle salad.

SERVES 4

per serving 5.1g fat; 1566kJ

serving suggestion Som tum, the Thai spicy-sour green pawpaw salad,
is a good, low-kilojoule accompaniment to the fish cakes.

tip Fish cakes can be made in advance and frozen; defrost in refrigerator
before cooking.

pesto fish kebabs

PREPARATION TIME 10 MINUTES • COOKING TIME 15 MINUTES

You can use any large fish fillets or steaks – such as ling, gemfish, snapper, kingfish or silver warehou – for this recipe. Soak eight bamboo skewers in water at least 1 hour before using to avoid scorching and splintering.

600g firm white fish fillets
1 tablespoon bottled pesto
1/2 cup loosely packed, finely chopped fresh flat-leaf parsley
1/2 small savoy cabbage (approximately 600g), shredded finely
1/3 cup (65g) drained baby capers
1 teaspoon finely grated lemon rind
1/2 cup loosely packed, finely chopped fresh mint leaves

1 Cut fish into 2cm cubes; combine with pesto and 1 tablespoon of the parsley in medium bowl. Thread onto eight skewers.

2 Cook kebabs, in batches, in heated large lightly oiled frying pan until browned and cooked as desired. Cover to keep warm.

3 Add cabbage to same heated pan; cook, stirring, until just tender. Stir in remaining parsley, capers, rind and mint.

4 Serve fish kebabs on stir-fried cabbage.

SERVES 4

per serving 5.2g fat; 813kJ
serving suggestion Serve with lemon-scented steamed rice.
tip Fish can be marinated and threaded onto skewers a day ahead; store, covered, in refrigerator.

cheese-crumbed fish fillets with stir-fried vegetables

PREPARATION TIME 15 MINUTES • COOKING TIME 15 MINUTES

You could use any firm-fleshed white fish fillets for this recipe – we used blue-eye. Make the breadcrumbs from bread that is at least a day old; grate or process stale bread to make crumbs.

1 cup (70g) stale wholemeal breadcrumbs
1/2 cup (45g) rolled oats
1 tablespoon drained capers, chopped finely
2 teaspoons finely grated lemon rind
1/4 cup (20g) finely grated romano cheese
1/4 cup loosely packed, finely chopped fresh flat-leaf parsley
1 tablespoon sesame oil
4 x 150g firm white fish fillets
1/2 cup (75g) plain flour
2 egg whites, beaten lightly
1 large carrot (180g), sliced finely
2 trimmed celery sticks (150g), sliced thinly
1 medium green capsicum (200g), sliced thinly
6 green onions, chopped finely
1 red thai chilli, seeded, chopped finely
1 tablespoon sesame seeds

1 Preheat oven to hot.

2 Combine breadcrumbs, oats, capers, rind, cheese, parsley and oil in medium bowl. Coat fish in flour, shake off excess; dip in egg, then in breadcrumb mixture.

3 Place fish, in single layer, in baking dish; bake, uncovered, in hot oven about 15 minutes or until cooked through.

4 Meanwhile, stir-fry carrot in heated large non-stick wok or frying pan. Add celery, capsicum, onion, chilli and sesame seeds; stir-fry until vegetables are just tender.

5 Serve sliced fish on stir-fried vegetables.

SERVES 4

per serving 11.9g fat; 1746kJ
serving suggestion Serve with wedges of lime or lemon.
tip Fish can be crumbed several hours ahead; store, covered, in refrigerator.

fish and zucchini stacks on tomato salad

PREPARATION TIME 15 MINUTES • COOKING TIME 10 MINUTES

You could use any firm, white-fleshed fish – ling, bream, snapper, blue-eye or silver warehou would be perfect for this recipe.

4 x 200g firm white fish fillets
2 medium green zucchini (240g)
2 medium yellow zucchini (240g)
4 medium tomatoes (760g), sliced thinly
1/3 cup (80ml) dry white wine
coarsely ground black pepper
2 tablespoons balsamic vinegar
2 tablespoons baby basil leaves

1 Preheat oven to very hot.

2 Halve fish pieces lengthways. Using vegetable peeler, peel zucchini into long thin ribbons.

3 Place four pieces of fish on large individual pieces of lightly oiled foil; top with zucchini ribbons then remaining fish pieces. Cut eight slices of tomato in half; place four half-slices on top of each stack. Drizzle stacks with wine; sprinkle with pepper.

4 Fold foil to enclose fish stacks; place in single layer in baking dish. Bake in very hot oven about 10 minutes or until fish is cooked through.

5 Divide remaining tomato slices equally among serving plates; top with unwrapped fish stacks. Drizzle stacks with vinegar; sprinkle with basil.

SERVES 4

per serving 5g fat; 1099kJ
serving suggestion Serve with a green salad and steamed potatoes.
tip Fish stacks can be assembled and wrapped in foil several hours ahead; store in refrigerator.

thai fish parcels

PREPARATION TIME 10 MINUTES • COOKING TIME 15 MINUTES

If you can't buy kaffir lime leaves, substitute the young leaves from any other citrus tree.

200g rice stick noodles
4 x 150g bream fillets
150g baby bok choy, quartered
150g snow peas, sliced thinly lengthways
1 tablespoon thinly sliced lemon grass
8 kaffir lime leaves, torn
1 teaspoon soy sauce
2 tablespoons sweet chilli sauce
1 teaspoon fish sauce
2 tablespoons lime juice
1 tablespoon coarsely chopped fresh coriander leaves

1 Preheat oven to hot.

2 Place noodles in large heatproof bowl; cover with boiling water. Stand until just tender; drain.

3 Divide noodles into four equal portions; place each on a large piece of foil. Top noodles with fish; top fish with equal amounts of bok choy, snow peas, lemon grass and lime leaves. Drizzle with combined sauces and juice. Enclose fish stacks in foil; place in single layer on oven tray.

4 Cook fish stacks in hot oven 15 minutes or until fish is cooked through; open foil and transfer stacks to serving plates. Sprinkle with coriander.

SERVES 4

per serving 4.4g fat; 1393kJ

serving suggestion Serve with wedges of lime or a salad made from fresh pomelo or grapefruit segments.

tip Fish parcels can be assembled several hours ahead; store in refrigerator.

ham and asparagus grill

PREPARATION TIME 10 MINUTES
COOKING TIME 10 MINUTES

340g can asparagus, drained
1 long loaf pide
2 medium tomatoes (380g), sliced
200g low-fat shaved ham
2 tablespoons coarsely chopped fresh basil leaves
1 small red onion (100g), sliced thinly
1 cup (100g) coarsely grated low-fat
  mozzarella cheese

1 Place asparagus in small bowl; mash with fork until almost smooth.

2 Quarter bread; split pieces horizontally. Toast both sides.

3 Divide remaining ingredients among the eight pieces of toast, finishing with cheese; cook under hot grill until cheese melts.

SERVES 4

per serving 9.2g fat; 1623kJ

tuna and tomato toasts

PREPARATION TIME 10 MINUTES
COOKING TIME 5 MINUTES

1 tablespoon drained capers, chopped finely
2 teaspoons finely chopped fresh dill tips
2 teaspoons olive oil
2 tablespoons lemon juice
1 long loaf pide
4 medium tomatoes (760g), seeded, sliced thinly
4 green onions, sliced thinly
2 x 125g cans smoked tuna slices
  in springwater, drained

1 Combine capers, dill, oil and juice in small bowl.

2 Quarter bread; split pieces horizontally. Toast both sides.

3 Divide combined tomato and onion among the eight pieces of toast; top with tuna. Drizzle with caper mixture.

SERVES 4

per serving 4.5g fat; 1317kJ

Left to right: vegetable grill; tuna and tomato toasts; ham and asparagus grill.

vegetable grill

PREPARATION TIME 25 MINUTES (plus standing time)
COOKING TIME 30 MINUTES

3 large carrots(540g),
  chopped coarsely
¼ cup (60ml) buttermilk
2 teaspoons ground cumin
2 teaspoons ground coriander
2 large red capsicums (700g)
4 baby eggplants (240g), sliced thinly
1 large red onion (300g),
  sliced thickly
180g mushrooms, sliced thickly
400g can artichoke hearts, drained,
  chopped coarsely
1 long loaf pide
1 cup (125g) coarsely grated
  low-fat cheddar cheese

1 Boil, steam or microwave carrot until just tender; drain. Blend or process carrot with buttermilk until smooth.

2 Cook spices in small dry heated frying pan until fragrant. Combine with carrot mixture; cover to keep warm.

3 Quarter capsicums; remove seeds and membranes. Roast under grill or in very hot oven, skin-side up, until skin blisters and blackens; cover capsicum pieces with plastic or paper for 5 minutes. Peel away skin; slice capsicum thickly.

4 Cook eggplant, onion, mushrooms and artichoke, in batches, on heated oiled grill plate (or grill or barbecue) until browned and just tender.

5 Quarter bread, split pieces horizontally; toast both sides.

6 Divide carrot mixture equally among the eight pieces of toast; top with capsicum, eggplant, mushrooms and artichoke. Sprinkle cheese equally over pieces; cook under hot grill until cheese melts.

SERVES 4

per serving 6.4g fat; 1762kJ

snacks

These between-meal snacks will satisfy the heartiest of appetites — and your waistline won't suffer for it.

100

desserts

We're wheeling out a luscious-looking sweets trolley in this chapter, one groaning with such delicious time- and waist-saving recipes that you'll have no problem fulfilling your friends' and family's craving for a happy ending.

satsuma plum clafouti

PREPARATION TIME 15 MINUTES • COOKING TIME 40 MINUTES

Sometimes called Indian blood plum, the large plum used in this recipe has a distinctive dark-red to purple fibrous flesh, is extremely juicy and pleasantly sweet, and is the plum most frequently canned.

1½ cups (375ml) low-fat custard
¼ cup (35g) self-raising flour
1 egg yolk
2 egg whites
825g can whole plums, drained, halved, seeded
2 teaspoons icing sugar mixture

1 Preheat oven to moderate.

2 Combine custard, flour and egg yolk in medium bowl.

3 Beat egg whites in small bowl of electric mixer on highest speed until soft peaks form; fold gently into custard mixture. Pour into 24cm-round ovenproof pie dish.

4 Pat plums dry with absorbent paper, arrange plums, cut-side down, over custard. Place pie dish on oven tray.

5 Bake in moderate oven, uncovered, about 40 minutes or until firm.

6 Just before serving, dust with sifted icing sugar.

SERVES 4

per serving 2.6g fat; 1019kJ
serving suggestion Serve with a scoop of low-fat ice-cream.
tip Canned apricots or peaches can be substituted for plums.

creamed rice with rhubarb and raspberries

PREPARATION TIME 10 MINUTES • COOKING TIME 1 HOUR

The Greeks invented the partnership of rice and milk for dessert.
They call it rizógalo; we call it seriously good comfort food.

1 litre (4 cups) skim milk
2/3 cup (150g) caster sugar
1/2 cup (100g) calrose rice
500g rhubarb, trimmed,
  chopped coarsely
1/4 cup (55g) caster
  sugar, extra
200g raspberries

1 Combine milk and sugar in medium saucepan; bring to a boil. Stir in rice; reduce heat. Simmer, covered, about 1 hour or until rice is creamy, stirring occasionally with wooden spoon.

2 Meanwhile, combine rhubarb and extra sugar in large saucepan. Cook over low heat, stirring, about 10 minutes or until rhubarb is tender.

3 Layer creamed rice and rhubarb mixture in serving dishes, finishing with rhubarb; sprinkle with raspberries.

SERVES 4

per serving 0.7g fat; 1852kJ

tips Any berry – boysenberries, blackberries, strawberries – can be substituted for the raspberrries.

A pinch of grated nutmeg or ground cardamom can be added to the creamed mixture.

mocha self-saucing pudding

PREPARATION TIME 10 MINUTES • COOKING TIME 45 MINUTES

Originally the name of a Middle-Eastern seaport from which premium Arabic coffee was exported, the word mocha has evolved to describe the serendipitous combination of coffee and chocolate.

1 cup (150g) self-raising flour
1/3 cup (35g) cocoa powder
3/4 cup (165g) caster sugar
**2 1/2 teaspoons instant
 coffee powder**
1/2 cup (125ml) skim milk
1 tablespoon vegetable oil
**1/2 cup (100g) firmly packed
 brown sugar**
1 1/4 cups (310ml) boiling water
1 tablespoon icing sugar mixture

1 Preheat oven to moderately slow.

2 Sift flour, 2 tablespoons of the cocoa, sugar and 2 teaspoons of the coffee powder into 1.25-litre (5-cup) ovenproof dish; gradually stir in milk and oil.

3 Sift brown sugar, remaining cocoa and remaining coffee evenly over flour mixture; gently pour the water over brown sugar mixture. Bake pudding, uncovered, in moderately slow oven about 45 minutes; serve dusted with sifted icing sugar.

SERVES 4

per serving 6.3g fat; 2073kJ

serving suggestion Raspberries or blueberries with thick cream make a good accompaniment.

tip This pudding is best served hot because the sauce is quickly absorbed by the pudding.

lemon cakes with passionfruit syrup

PREPARATION TIME 10 MINUTES • COOKING TIME 25 MINUTES

You will need about six passionfruit to make this recipe. The thin-skinned purple-black variety will yield much more pulp than the thicker-skinned Panama passionfruit.

1¼ cups (185g) self-raising flour
½ cup (110g) caster sugar
2 teaspoons finely grated lemon rind
1 egg, beaten lightly
40g butter, melted
2 tablespoons skim milk
¾ cup (210g) low-fat yogurt
1 cup (250ml) water
1 teaspoon cornflour
½ cup (125ml) passionfruit pulp
2 tablespoons finely sliced lemon rind

1 Preheat oven to moderate.

2 Grease eight holes of a 12-hole (⅓ cup/80ml) muffin pan.

3 Combine flour in medium bowl with ¼ cup of the sugar and grated rind. Add egg, butter, milk and yogurt; stir until just combined. Divide mixture among prepared pan holes; bake in moderate oven about 25 minutes. Stand cakes in pan 5 minutes; turn out onto wire rack.

4 Meanwhile, combine the water and remaining sugar in small saucepan. Stir over heat until sugar dissolves; bring to a boil. Reduce heat; simmer, uncovered, without stirring, 10 minutes. Stir in blended cornflour and passionfruit until mixture boils and thickens. Strain into small heatproof jug; discard seeds. Stir in sliced rind; cool. Serve lemon cakes with passionfruit syrup.

MAKES 8

per muffin 5.1g fat; 822kJ

serving suggestion You could scatter a few berries, such as blueberries or raspberries, on each serving plate.

tip Lime rind can be substituted for lemon rind.

pineapple crunch

PREPARATION TIME 10 MINUTES • COOKING TIME 20 MINUTES

We used Just Right breakfast cereal in this recipe but you can use any flake and dried fruit cereal, even a muesli or granola-like product.

850g can crushed pineapple, drained
2 small nashis (360g), chopped coarsely
1 tablespoon Malibu liqueur
3 cups (150g) Just Right
2 tablespoons pepitas
2 tablespoons sunflower seeds
1/3 cup (95g) low-fat yogurt
2 tablespoons honey

1 Preheat oven to moderate.

2 Grease four 1-cup (250ml) ovenproof dishes; place on oven tray.

3 Combine pineapple, nashi and Malibu in medium bowl; divide among prepared dishes.

4 Using one hand, crumble cereal in same bowl; stir in seeds, yogurt and honey. Divide mixture among prepared dishes; bake, uncovered, in moderate oven about 20 minutes or until browned lightly.

SERVES 4

per serving 8g fat; 1713kJ

serving suggestion Serve topped with low-fat yogurt or low-fat ice-cream and a dollop of fresh passionfruit pulp or drizzle of honey.

tip You can substitute chopped, drained canned peaches or apricots for the pineapple in this recipe.

ricotta and berry trifle

PREPARATION TIME 15 MINUTES

The traditional English favourite is given a new look with this summery update. If you prefer, trifle can be served in a large glass bowl. Pavlova nests are commercially made small meringue shells sold in packages of 10.

200g raspberries
200g blueberries
200g strawberries, quartered
2 cups (400g) low-fat
   ricotta cheese
1/3 cup (80ml) orange juice
1/3 cup (80ml) maple syrup
2 pavlova nests (20g), crumbled
1 tablespoon toasted
   flaked almonds

1 Combine berries in medium bowl.

2 Blend or process combined cheese, juice and maple syrup until smooth.

3 Divide a quarter of the cheese mixture among four 1-cup (250ml) dessert glasses; sprinkle with some of the berries. Repeat layering with remaining cheese mixture and berries, finishing with berries.

4 Sprinkle meringue and nuts over trifles. Refrigerate, covered, for at least 3 hours.

SERVES 4

per serving 11g fat; 1226kJ

serving suggestion You can drizzle some pureed berries over the top of the trifles.

apple and fig bread pudding

PREPARATION TIME 20 MINUTES • COOKING TIME 50 MINUTES

Granny smith and golden delicious are the best apple varieties to use for this recipe.

2 tablespoons honey
2 tablespoons water
8 slices white bread
1 medium apple (150g), cored,
  quartered, sliced thinly
12 dried figs (200g), halved
2 cups (500ml) skim milk
2 eggs
2 tablespoons caster sugar
1/2 teaspoon ground cinnamon
2 teaspoons icing sugar mixture

1 Preheat oven to moderately slow. Stir honey and the water in small
  saucepan over low heat until honey melts.

2 Cut crusts from bread; discard crusts. Halve slices diagonally; brush
  both sides of bread with honey mixture. Layer bread, apple and fig,
  overlapping pieces slightly, in lightly greased shallow rectangular
  1.25-litre (5 cup) ovenproof dish.

3 Whisk milk, eggs and sugar together in medium bowl; strain into large
  jug, skimming and discarding any foam. Pour half the milk mixture over
  the bread; stand 5 minutes. Pour over remaining milk mixture; sprinkle
  with cinnamon.

4 Place dish in large baking dish; add enough boiling water to come
  halfway up sides of dish. Bake pudding, uncovered, in moderately slow
  oven about 45 minutes or until top is browned lightly and pudding is set.
  Dust with sifted icing sugar before serving.

SERVES 4

per serving 3g fat; 1185kJ

serving suggestion A dollop of low-fat yogurt, flavoured with honey and
cinnamon, or some fresh raspberries makes a good accompaniment.

tip Remove bread and butter pudding from water bath immediately after
cooking to prevent it from overcooking and becoming tough.

chocolate mousse

PREPARATION TIME 5 MINUTES (plus refrigeration time)

We used Baileys Original Irish Cream, based on Irish whiskey, spirits and cream, in this recipe. Frûche is a commercial dessert having less than 0.5g fat per 100g; substitute fromage frais or a low-fat yogurt if you cannot find it.

**2 teaspoons instant
 coffee powder
1 teaspoon hot water
120g dark chocolate, melted
400g french vanilla
 low-fat Frûche
1 tablespoon irish
 cream liqueur**

1 Combine coffee with the water in medium bowl, stirring until coffee dissolves. Add chocolate, Frûche and liqueur, stirring, until combined.

2 Divide among four ³/₄-cup (180ml) serving dishes; refrigerate, covered, about 30 minutes or until firm.

SERVES 4

per serving 9.1g fat; 1072kJ

serving suggestion Raspberries, strawberries or blueberries are an appealing accompaniment to this mousse.

tip Mousse can be prepared a day ahead; store, covered, in refrigerator until just before serving.

caramelised oranges with ice-cream

PREPARATION TIME 10 MINUTES • COOKING TIME 10 MINUTES

Navel or jaffa (Spanish) oranges are ideal for this recipe because they have very few seeds.

4 large oranges (1.2kg)
2 tablespoons brown sugar
2 tablespoons Grand Marnier
200g low-fat vanilla ice-cream

1 Peel oranges, removing as much white pith as possible; cut crossways into thick slices.

2 Place orange, in single layer, on oven tray. Sprinkle with sugar; drizzle with liqueur. Cook orange on both sides under hot grill until just caramelised.

3 Divide ice-cream and orange among four serving dishes; drizzle with pan juices.

SERVES 4

per serving 3.2g fat; 898kJ

serving suggestion Sprinkle some finely chopped mint or purple basil over the oranges.

tip Cointreau or Triple Sec can be substituted for Grand Marnier.

apple and cinnamon pancakes with maple syrup

PREPARATION TIME 20 MINUTES • COOKING TIME 20 MINUTES

Maple syrup, the processed sap of the maple tree, has a natural affinity with apple. Maple-flavoured syrup or pancake syrup, made from cane sugar and artificial maple flavouring, is not an adequate substitute.

1 cup (150g) self-raising flour
¹/₄ cup (50g) firmly packed
  brown sugar
¹/₂ teaspoon ground cinnamon
¹/₂ cup (125ml) skim milk
1 egg yolk
¹/₂ cup (110g) canned pie apple,
  chopped coarsely
2 egg whites
2 granny smith apples, peeled,
  cored, cut into wedges
2 tablespoons brown sugar, extra
200g low-fat vanilla ice-cream
2 tablespoons maple syrup

1 Combine flour in large bowl with sugar, cinnamon, milk, egg yolk and canned pie apple.

2 Beat egg whites in small bowl of electric mixer on highest speed until soft peaks form; fold gently into apple mixture.

3 Heat medium non-stick frying pan; pour in ¹/₄-cup amounts of batter for each pancake. Cook until browned both sides; repeat with remaining batter. You will have eight pancakes.

4 Cook apple wedges and extra sugar over low heat in same pan, stirring, until apple caramelises.

5 Divide pancakes among serving dishes. Top with apple mixture then ice-cream; drizzle with maple syrup.

SERVES 4

per serving 2.1g fat; 1157kJ

serving suggestion A flavoured ice-cream, such as toffee crunch or butterscotch, can be used instead of plain vanilla; omit the maple syrup if you use a flavoured ice-cream.

glossary

all-bran a low-fat, high-fibre breakfast cereal based on wheat bran.

almond
BLANCHED skins removed.

FLAKED paper-thin slices.

GROUND also known as almond meal.

MEAL also known as finely ground almonds; powdered to a flour-like texture.

PASTE we used almond-flavoured cake paste or prepared marzipan.

SLIVERED small lengthways-cut pieces.

bacon rashers also known as slices of bacon; made from pork side, cured and smoked.

baking powder a raising agent consisting mainly of two parts cream of tartar to one part bicarbonate of soda (baking soda).

barley flakes flattened grains produced by steaming the barley grain then rolling it into flakes.

beef
EYE FILLET tenderloin.

MINCE also known as ground beef.

RIB-EYE available as steak and whole piece for roasting. A tender cut also known as scotch fillet.

RUMP STEAK boneless tender cut.

beetroot also known as beets.

bicarbonate of soda also known as baking or carb soda.

bok choy also called pak choi or Chinese white cabbage; has a fresh, mild mustard taste. Baby bok choy is also available.

breadcrumbs
PACKAGED fine-textured, crunchy, purchased, white breadcrumbs.

STALE one- or two-day-old bread made into crumbs by grating, blending or processing.

burghul also known as bulghur wheat; hulled steamed wheat kernels that are dried and crushed.

butter use salted or unsalted ("sweet") butter; 125g is equal to one stick of butter.

celeriac root vegetable with brown skin, white flesh and a celery-like flavour.

cheese
CHEDDAR a semi-hard cow-milk cheese; we used a low fat variety with a fat content of not more than 7%.

CREAM mild-flavoured fresh cheese made of cow milk; we used one with 21% fat.

FETTA salty white cheese made from cow milk, though sheep- and goat-milk varieties are available. We used low-fat fetta with 15% fat content.

MOZZARELLA soft, spun-curd cheese traditionally made from water buffalo milk; cow-milk versions of this product, commonly known as pizza cheese, are available. We used a version with 17.5% fat.

PARMESAN also known as parmigiano, parmesan is a hard, grainy cow-milk cheese which originated in Italy. Parmigiano reggiano is generally aged longer than grana padano.

RICOTTA a low-fat, fresh unripened cheese made from whey with 8.5% fat.

ROMANO hard sheep- or cow-milk cheese; straw-coloured and grainy in texture.

chicken
BREAST FILLET breast halved, skinned and boned.

MINCE also known as ground chicken.

TENDERLOIN thin strip of meat lying just under the breast.

THIGH FILLET thigh from which the skin and bones have been removed.

chickpeas also called garbanzos, hummus or channa; an irregularly round, sandy-coloured legume.

chillies available in many different types and sizes. Use rubber gloves when chopping and seeding fresh chillies as they can burn your skin. Removing seeds lessens the heat level.

chinese broccoli also known as gai lum.

chinese cabbage also known as Peking cabbage or wong bok.

choy sum also known as flowering bok choy or flowering white cabbage.

ciabatta in Italian, the word means slipper, which is the traditional shape of this crisp-crusted white bread.

coconut milk we used a canned light coconut milk with a fat content of less than 6%.

cooking-oil spray we used a cholesterol-free cooking spray made from canola oil.

cornflour also known as cornstarch; used as a thickening agent in cooking.

cornmeal ground dried corn (maize); available in different textures.

couscous a fine, grain-like cereal product, made from semolina.

curry paste
MASALA literally meaning blended spices; a masala can be whole spices, a paste or a powder, and can include herbs as well as spices and other seasonings. Traditional dishes are usually named after particular masalas.

TANDOORI consists of garlic, tamarind, ginger, coriander, chilli, spices and sometimes red food colouring.

eggplant purple-skinned vegetable also known as aubergine.

essences also known as extracts; generally the by-product of distillation of plants.

five-spice powder a fragrant mixture of ground cinnamon, cloves, star anise, Sichuan pepper and fennel seeds.

flour
BUCKWHEAT although not a true cereal, flour is made from its seeds. Available from health food stores.

PLAIN an all-purpose flour, made from wheat.

SELF-RAISING plain flour combined with baking powder in the proportion of 1 cup flour to 2 teaspoons baking powder.

fruche commercial dessert with less than 0.5g fat per 100g. Similar to fromage frais.

chinese cabbage

baby bok choy

choy sum

pitta bread

garam masala a blend of spices, originating in North India; based on varying proportions of cardamom, cinnamon, cloves, coriander, fennel and cumin, roasted and ground together.

ginger, fresh also known as green or root ginger; the thick gnarled root of a tropical plant. Can be kept, peeled, covered with dry sherry in a jar and refrigerated, or frozen in an airtight container.

golden syrup a by-product of refined sugarcane; pure maple syrup or honey can be substituted.

grand marnier orange-flavoured liqueur.

ham we used light ham which has a fat content of approximately 4% – about half that of regular leg ham.

irish cream we used Baileys Original Irish Cream, based on Irish whiskey, spirits and cream.

just right breakfast cereal containing wheat flakes, rolled oats, rye, sultanas and dried apricots.

kaffir lime
FRUIT medium-sized citrus fruit with wrinkly yellow-green skin, used in Thai cooking.
LEAVES aromatic leaves used fresh or dried in Asian dishes.

kumara Polynesian name of orange-fleshed sweet potato often confused with yam.

lamb
CUTLET small, tender rib chop.
FILLET tenderloin; the smaller piece of meat from a row of loin chops or cutlets.

lamington pan 20cm x 30cm slab cake pan, 3cm deep.

lavash flat, unleavened bread that originated in the Mediterranean.

lemon grass a tall, clumping, lemon-smelling and -tasting, sharp-edged grass; the white lower part of each stem is chopped and used in Asian cooking.

lentils dried pulses often identified by and named after their colour; also known as dhal.

low-fat custard we used trim custard with 0.9% fat.

low-fat ice cream we used an ice-cream with 3% fat.

low-fat mayonnaise we used cholesterol-free mayonnaise with 3% fat.

low-fat sour cream we used light sour cream with 18.5% fat.

low-fat thickened cream we used thickened cream with 18% fat.

low-fat yogurt we used yogurt with a fat content of less than 0.2%.

malibu coconut-flavoured rum.

maple syrup distilled sap of the maple tree. Maple-flavoured syrup or pancake syrup is made from cane sugar and artificial maple flavouring and is not an adequate substitute for the real thing.

melons
ROCKMELON oval melon with orange flesh; also known as a cantaloupe.
WATERMELON large green-skinned melon with crisp, juicy, deep pink flesh.
HONEYDEW an oval melon with delicate taste and pale-green flesh.

mesclun mixed baby salad leaves also sold as salad mix or gourmet salad mix; a mixture of assorted young lettuce and other green leaves.

milk
BUTTERMILK despite the implication of its name, is low in fat. Commercially made, by a method similar to yogurt. A good low-fat substitute for cream or sour cream.
SKIM we used milk with 0.15% fat content or lower.

mince meat also known as ground meat.

mushrooms
BUTTON small, cultivated white mushrooms having a delicate, subtle flavour.
SWISS BROWN light to dark brown mushrooms with full-bodied flavour. Button or cup mushrooms can be substituted for Swiss brown mushrooms.
OYSTER also known as abalone; grey-white fan-shaped mushroom.

noodles
FRESH RICE thick, wide, almost white in colour; made from rice and vegetable oil. Must be covered with boiling water to remove starch and excess oil before using in soups and stir-fries.
HOKKIEN also known as stir-fry noodles; fresh egg noodles resembling thick, yellow-brown spaghetti needing no pre-cooking before being used.
RICE STICK a dried noodle, available flat and wide or very thin; made from rice flour and water.

onions
BROWN AND WHITE are interchangeable. Their pungent flesh adds flavour to a vast range of dishes.
GREEN also known as scallion or (incorrectly) shallot; an immature onion picked before the bulb has formed, having a long, green edible stalk.
RED also known as Spanish, red Spanish or Bermuda onion; a sweet-flavoured, large, purple-red onion.

pappadums sun-dried wafers made from lentil and rice flours, oil and spices.

parsley, flat-leaf also known as continental parsley or Italian parsley.

passionfruit also known as granadilla; a small tropical fruit, native to Brazil, comprised of a tough outer skin surrounding edible black sweet-sour seeds.

patty-pan squash yellow baby squash also known as patty-pan, summer squash or scaloppine. Yellow or green thin-skinned squash.

kaffir limes and leaves

lemon grass

pecan nut native to the United States and now grown locally; golden-brown, buttery and rich.

pepitas dried pumpkin seeds.

pide also known as Turkish bread, comes in long (about 45cm) flat loaves as well as individual rounds; made from wheat flour and sprinkled with sesame or black onion seeds.

pitta (Lebanese bread) also spelled pita, this wheat-flour pocket bread is sold in large, flat pieces that separate easily into two thin rounds. Also available in small thick pieces called pocket pitta.

polenta cereal made of ground corn (maize); also the name of the dish made from it.

popping corn a variety of corn that is sold as kernels.

pork

FILLET skinless, boneless eye-fillet cut from the loin.

MINCE also known as ground pork.

STEAK also known as schnitzel; thin slices cut from the leg or rump.

raisins large, dark brown dried sweet grapes.

rhubarb a vegetable; only the firm, reddish stems are eaten.

rice

ARBORIO small, round grain rice well-suited to absorb a large amount of liquid.

BASMATI RICE a white fragrant long-grain rice.

BROWN natural whole grain.

CALROSE medium-grain; can be used instead of long- or short-grain varieties.

JASMINE fragrant long-grained rice.

LONG-GRAIN elongated grain, remains separate when cooked.

WILD blackish brown seed from North America is not a member of the rice family. It is fairly expensive as it's difficult to cultivate but has a delicious nutty flavour.

rice flakes available from supermarkets and health food stores; also known as parva in India.

rice paper sheets mostly from Vietnam (banh trang). Made from rice paste and stamped into rounds, with a woven pattern. Store well at room temperature, but are quite brittle and will break if dropped. Dipped in water, they become pliable wrappers for fried food and for eating fresh (uncooked) vegetables.

pepitas

rolled oats, traditional whole oat grains that have been steamed and flattened. Not the quick-cook variety.

rye flakes flat flakes of crushed rye grain.

sauces

FISH also called nam pla or nuoc nam; made from salted pulverised fermented fish, usually anchovies. Has strong taste and pungent smell.

HOISIN SAUCE a thick, sweet and spicy Chinese paste made from salted fermented soy beans, onions and garlic; used as a marinade or baste, or to accent stir-fries and barbecued or roasted foods.

KETJAP MANIS Indonesian sweet, thick soy sauce which has sugar and spices added.

OYSTER Asian in origin, this sauce is made from oysters and their brine, cooked with salt and soy sauce, and thickened with starches.

SATAY traditional Indonesian/Malaysian spicy peanut sauce served with grilled meat skewers. Make your own or buy one of the many packaged versions easily obtained from supermarkets or specialty Asian food stores.

SOY made from fermented soy beans; several varieties are available in supermarkets and Asian food stores.

SWEET CHILLI a comparatively mild, Thai-type sauce made from red chillies, sugar, garlic and vinegar.

TERIYAKI a homemade or commercially bottled sauce usually made from soy sauce, mirin, sugar, ginger and other spices; it imparts a distinctive glaze when brushed on meat to be grilled.

TOMATO PASTA SAUCE, BOTTLED prepared sauce available from supermarkets; sometimes labelled sugo.

TABASCO brand name of an extremely fiery sauce made from vinegar, hot red peppers and salt.

sesame

SEEDS black and white are the most common of the oval seeds harvested from the tropical plant *Sesamum indicum*; however there are red and brown varieties also. Used in za'atar, halva and tahini and a good source of calcium. To toast, spread seeds evenly on oven tray, toast in moderate oven briefly.

OIL made from roasted, crushed, white sesame seeds; a flavouring rather than a cooking medium.

soy wholegrain flakes calcium-rich flakes made from soy beans.

sugar we used coarse granulated table sugar, also known as crystal sugar, unless otherwise specified.

BROWN a soft, fine sugar retaining molasses.

CASTER also known as superfine or finely granulated table sugar.

ICING SUGAR MIXTURE also known as confectioners' sugar or powdered sugar; granulated sugar crushed together with a small amount (about 3%) cornflour added.

PALM very fine sugar from the coconut palm. It is sold in cakes, also known as gula jawa, gula melaka and jaggery. Palm sugar can be substituted with brown or black sugar.

PURE ICING SUGAR also known as confectioners' sugar or powdered sugar.

RAW natural brown granulated sugar.

sultanas small dried grapes, also known as golden raisins.

sunflower seeds kernels from dried husked sunflower seeds.

tofu also known as bean curd, an off-white, custard-like product made from the milk of crushed soy beans; comes fresh as soft or firm, and processed as fried or pressed dried sheets. Leftover fresh tofu can be refrigerated in water (which is changed daily) up to 4 days. Silken tofu refers to the method by which it is made – where it is strained through silk.

tortilla unleavened bread sold frozen, fresh or vacuum-packed; made from wheat flour or corn (maize meal).

triticale a nutritious hybrid of wheat (triticum) and rye (secale) which contains more protein and less gluten than wheat and has nutty sweet flavour. Available in whole grain, flour and flakes.

unprocessed bran made from the outer layer of a cereal, usually the husks of wheat, rice or oats.

veal meat from a young calf.

CHOP from the rib and loin (back).

STEAK thinly sliced cut also known as schnitzel.

vinegar

BALSAMIC authentic only from the province of Modena, Italy; made from a regional wine of white Trebbiano grapes specially processed then aged in antique wooden casks to give the exquisite pungent flavour.

RED WINE based on fermented red wine.

WHITE made from spirit of cane sugar.

WHITE WINE made from white wine.

wheat germ small creamy flakes milled from the embryo of the wheat.

zucchini also known as courgette.

sesame seeds

index

make your own stock

These recipes can be made up to 4 days ahead and stored, covered, in the refrigerator. Be sure to remove any fat from the surface after the cooled stock has been refrigerated overnight. If the stock is to be kept longer, it is best to freeze it in smaller quantities.
All stock recipes make about 2.5 litres (10 cups).

Stock is also available in cans or tetra packs. Stock cubes or powder can be used. As a guide, 1 teaspoon of stock powder or 1 small crumbled stock cube mixed with 1 cup (250ml) water will give a fairly strong stock. Be aware of the salt and fat content of stock cubes and powders and prepared stocks.

BEEF STOCK

2kg meaty beef bones
2 medium onions (300g)
2 sticks celery, chopped
2 medium carrots (250g), chopped
3 bay leaves
2 teaspoons black peppercorns
5 litres (20 cups) water
3 litres (12 cups) water, extra

Place bones and unpeeled chopped onions in baking dish. Bake in hot oven about 1 hour or until bones and onions are well browned. Transfer bones and onions to large pan, add celery, carrots, bay leaves, peppercorns and water, simmer, uncovered, 3 hours. Add extra water, simmer, uncovered, further 1 hour; strain.

CHICKEN STOCK

2kg chicken bones
2 medium onions (300g), chopped
2 sticks celery, chopped
2 medium carrots (250g), chopped
3 bay leaves
2 teaspoons black peppercorns
5 litres (20 cups) water

Combine all ingredients in large pan, simmer, uncovered, 2 hours; strain.

FISH STOCK

1.5kg fish bones
3 litres (12 cups) water
1 medium onion (150g), chopped
2 sticks celery, chopped
2 bay leaves
1 teaspoon black peppercorns

Combine all ingredients in large pan, simmer, uncovered, 20 minutes; strain.

VEGETABLE STOCK

2 large carrots (360g), chopped
2 large parsnips (360g), chopped
4 medium onions (600g), chopped
12 sticks celery, chopped
4 bay leaves
2 teaspoons black peppercorns
6 litres (24 cups) water

Combine all ingredients in large pan, simmer, uncovered, 1½ hours; strain.

facts and figures

Wherever you live, you'll be able to use our recipes with the help of these easy-to-follow conversions. While these conversions are approximate only, the difference between an exact and the approximate conversion of various liquid and dry measures is but minimal and will not affect your cooking results.

dry measures

metric	imperial
15g	1/2oz
30g	1oz
60g	2oz
90g	3oz
125g	4oz (1/4lb)
155g	5oz
185g	6oz
220g	7oz
250g	8oz (1/2lb)
280g	9oz
315g	10oz
345g	11oz
375g	12oz (3/4lb)
410g	13oz
440g	14oz
470g	15oz
500g	16oz (1lb)
750g	24oz (1 1/2lb)
1kg	32oz (2lb)

liquid measures

metric	imperial
30ml	1 fluid oz
60ml	2 fluid oz
100ml	3 fluid oz
125ml	4 fluid oz
150ml	5 fluid oz (1/4 pint/1 gill)
190ml	6 fluid oz
250ml	8 fluid oz
300ml	10 fluid oz (1/2 pint)
500ml	16 fluid oz
600ml	20 fluid oz (1 pint)
1000ml (1 litre)	1 3/4 pints

helpful measures

metric	imperial
3mm	1/8in
6mm	1/4in
1cm	1/2in
2cm	3/4in
2.5cm	1in
5cm	2in
6cm	2 1/2in
8cm	3in
10cm	4in
13cm	5in
15cm	6in
18cm	7in
20cm	8in
23cm	9in
25cm	10in
28cm	11in
30cm	12in (1ft)

oven temperatures

These oven temperatures are only a guide. Always check the manufacturer's manual.

	°C (Celsius)	°F (Fahrenheit)	Gas Mark
Very slow	120	250	1
Slow	150	300	2
Moderately slow	160	325	3
Moderate	180 - 190	350 - 375	4
Moderately hot	200 - 210	400 - 425	5
Hot	220 - 230	450 - 475	6
Very hot	240 - 250	500 - 525	7

helpful measures

The difference between one country's measuring cups and another's is, at most, within a 2 or 3 teaspoon variance. (For the record, 1 Australian metric measuring cup holds approximately 250ml.) The most accurate way of measuring dry ingredients is to weigh them. When measuring liquids, use a clear glass or plastic jug with the metric markings. (One Australian metric tablespoon holds 20ml; one Australian metric teaspoon holds 5ml.)

If you would like to purchase *The Australian Women's Weekly* Test Kitchen's metric measuring cups and spoons (as approved by Standards Australia), turn to page 120 for details and order coupon. You will receive:

- a graduated set of 4 cups for measuring dry ingredients, with sizes marked on the cups.
- a graduated set of 4 spoons for measuring dry and liquid ingredients, with amounts marked on the spoons.

Note: North America, NZ and the UK use 15ml tablespoons. All cup and spoon measurements are level.

We use large eggs having an average weight of 60g.

how to measure

When using graduated metric measuring cups, shake dry ingredients loosely into the appropriate cup. Do not tap the cup on a bench or tightly pack the ingredients unless directed to do so. Level top of measuring cups and measuring spoons with a knife. When measuring liquids, place a clear glass or plastic jug with metric markings on a flat surface to check accuracy at eye level.

Looking after your interest...

Keep your Home Library cookbooks clean, tidy and within easy reach with slipcovers designed to hold up to 12 books. *Plus* you can follow our recipes perfectly with a set of accurate measuring cups and spoons, as used by *The Australian Women's Weekly* Test Kitchen.

TO ORDER

Mail or fax Photocopy or complete the coupon below and post to AWW Home Library Reader Offer, ACP Direct, PO Box 7036, Sydney NSW 1028, *or* fax to (02) 9267 4363.

Credit cards Have your details ready then, if you live in Sydney, phone 9260 0000; if you live elsewhere in Australia, phone 1800 252 515 (free call, Mon-Fri, 8.30am-5.30pm).

PRICE

Book Holder
Australia: $13.10 (incl. GST).
Elsewhere: $A21.95.

Metric Measuring Set
Australia: $6.50 (incl. GST).
New Zealand: $A8.00.
Elsewhere: $A9.95.
Prices include postage and handling.
This offer is available in all countries.

PAYMENT

Australian residents We accept the credit cards listed on the coupon, money orders and cheques.

Overseas residents We accept the credit cards listed on the coupon, drafts in $A drawn on an Australian bank, and also British, New Zealand and U.S. cheques in the currency of the country of issue. Credit card charges are at the exchange rate current at the time of payment.

✂

❑ **BOOK HOLDER**   ❑ **METRIC MEASURING SET**

Please indicate number(s) required.

Mr/Mrs/Ms _____

Address _____

_____

Postcode _____ Country _____

Ph: Bus. Hours:(   )_____

I enclose my cheque/money order for $ _____ payable to ACP Direct

OR: please charge my

❑ Bankcard ❑ Visa ❑ MasterCard ❑ Diners Club ❑ Amex

Expiry Date ____/____

Cardholder's signature _____

Please allow up to 30 days for delivery within Australia. Allow up to 6 weeks for overseas deliveries. Both offers expire 31/08/01.
HLGFF00